Kiet and the
Opium War

KIET AND THE OPIUM WAR

GARY ALEXANDER

ST. MARTIN'S PRESS
NEW YORK

The author apologizes to the Socialist Republic of the Union of Burma, the People's Republic of China, the Lao People's Democratic Republic, and the Kingdom of Thailand for geographic distortions and for encroachment on their borders. Tolerance is also asked for liberties taken with the topography and the climate of the region.

Library of Congress Cataloging-in-Publication Data

Alexander, Gary, 1941–
    Kiet and the opium war / by Gary Alexander.
        p.   cm.
    "A Thomas Dunne book."
    ISBN 0-312-05106-9
    I. Title.
PS3551.I3554K55   1990
813'.54—dc20
                                                            90-37325
                                                            CIP

First Edition
10 9 8 7 6 5 4 3 2 1

For Ruth Cavin and Al Hart,
Coconspirators

CAST OF CHARACTERS

BAMSAN KIET (bomb-sawn key-yet), Hickorn's superintendent of police

CAPTAIN BINH (bin), Kiet's adjutant

PRINCE NOVISAD PAKSE (nove-ih-said pock-see), ruler of Luong

QUIN CANH (quinn can), Kiet's lover

BAO CANH (bough can), Quin's son

LE CANH (lee can), Quin's mother

VINCENT "LITTLE BIG VINNIE" JONES, American gangster

CUONG VAN (cong van), Luong's minister of defense

TYLER POLK (TIP) TAYLOR, American drug enforcement adviser

SOUVANG ZHU (so-vang zoo), air vice-marshal, commander of Royal Luongan Air Force

LON MUOI (lon moo-ee), associate deputy minister of defense, Drug Enforcement Investigation

AMBASSADOR SHIHERAZADE, Soviet ambassador

ALBERTO FESTERRA, Cuban tropical agriculture expert

YUNG LIM (young limb), Luongan criminal

RIL THOI (rill toy), Luong Rouge leader

Religion is the opium of the people.
—KARL MARX

Opium is the opium of the people.
—BAMSAN KIET

Opium? What do I know from opium?
—VINCENT "LITTLE BIG VINNIE" JONES

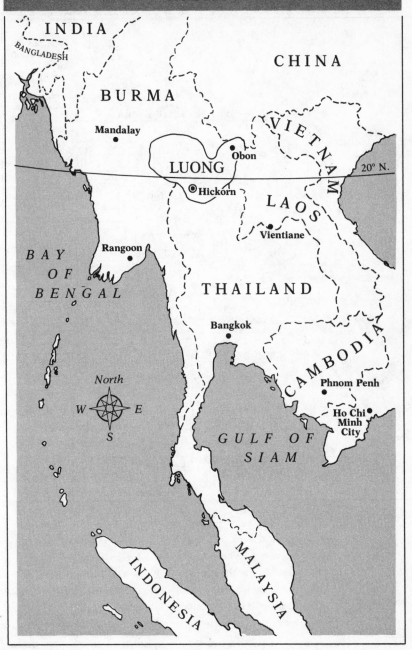

The Kingdom of LUONG

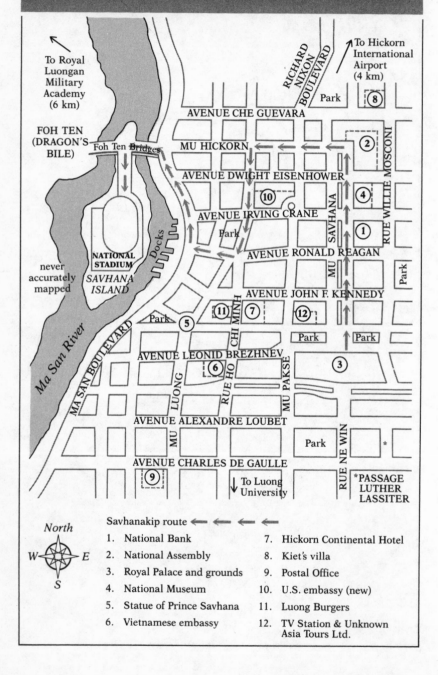

Downtown HICKORN

To Royal
Luongan
Military
Academy
(6 km)

To Hickorn
International
Airport
(4 km)

RICHARD NIXON BOULEVARD

Park

8

FOH TEN
(DRAGON'S
BILE)

Foh Ten Bridges

AVENUE CHE GUEVARA

MU HICKORN

2

AVENUE DWIGHT EISENHOWER

10

AVENUE IRVING CRANE

Park

4

1

RUE WILLIE MOSCONI

MU SAVHANA

NATIONAL
STADIUM

Docks

AVENUE RONALD REAGAN

never
accurately
mapped

SAVHANA
ISLAND

AVENUE JOHN F. KENNEDY

Park

Ma San River

MA SAN BOULEVARD

Park

5

11

RUE HO CHI MINH

7

12

Park

Park

AVENUE LEONID BREZHNEV

6

RUE HO CHI MINH

MU PAKSE

3

MU LUONG

AVENUE ALEXANDRE LOUBET

MU

Park

RUE NE WIN

AVENUE CHARLES DE GAULLE

9

To Luong
University

*PASSAGE
LUTHER
LASSITER

*

North

W — E

S

Savhanakip route ← ← ← ←

1. National Bank
2. National Assembly
3. Royal Palace and grounds
4. National Museum
5. Statue of Prince Savhana
6. Vietnamese embassy

7. Hickorn Continental Hotel
8. Kiet's villa
9. Postal Office
10. U.S. embassy (new)
11. Luong Burgers
12. TV Station & Unknown
    Asia Tours Ltd.

Prologue

Acceptance of the following is necessary for suspension of disbelief:

1. The Kingdom of Luong actually exists.

2. It is a remote Southeast Asian backwater surrounded by China, Burma, Laos, and Thailand.

3. It is the size and shape of Louisiana.

4. It has the gross national product of Baton Rouge.

5. It was granted independence by France in 1954.

6. It is a constitutional monarchy ruled by eighty-year-old Prince Novisad Pakse, a cagey neutralist who straddles the geopolitical fence by the simple act of naming and renaming the streets of the capital city, Hickorn, in honor of powerful foreigners.

7. Prince Pakse's abiding passion is pocket billiards and some regard him as a senile fool, but his country has managed to avoid the revolutionary turmoil suffered by Vietnam, Cambodia, and Laos.

8. Luong's northern highlands are wild and mountainous.

9. The river valleys and flatlands of the south are lush and tropical.

10. Luong's industrial base is negligible—cigarettes, beverages, bicycles, construction materials. These products are consumed domestically.

11. Agriculture is Luong's principal industry. Rice, tobacco, corn, coffee, and opium are grown.

12. Some rice is exported, but opium is Luong's only cash crop of note.

13. Hickorn, the capital, has a population of 225,000. It is located in the south, on the Ma San River. It is hot, humid, and formerly sleepy.

14. Hickorn's top law enforcement official is Superintendent of Police Bamsan Kiet.

15. Kiet's function is the same as that of police chiefs throughout the world: to control crime and to ensure the safety of inhabitants within his jurisdiction.

16. But events of the past several months have hampered the superintendent's ability to perform normal duties.

    a. A free-for-all opium war has diverted the customary Golden Triangle trafficking routes from Thailand and Burma to the Kingdom of Luong.

    b. Bamsan Kiet is in love.

1

A gentle tattoo against Kiet's ribs awakened him.

He had been nudged out of such a deep sleep that he needed a moment to realize where he was. Quin's apartment, yes. Her bed, oh, yes. But what time was it? The bedroom was black, no light penetrating draperies. Early? Late? Their naps following lovemaking were pleasurable disruptions of his normal sleep pattern, but Kiet often awoke disoriented.

"Bamsan," Quin whispered.

"Uh," Kiet said.

Satisfied that Kiet was conscious, Quin stopped elbowing him and sat up. "Do you hear it?"

Kiet caressed a soft, warm leg. "Huh?"

She discarded his arm and stood. "Shh. Listen."

He listened and heard a rhythmic thudding on the apartment door, the sound of a domestic animal scuffing its paw, begging to be let in. Kiet groaned. It had to be Le, Quin's mother. The old bat suffered a mild case of arthritis. To spare her inflamed knuckles, she was pounding with the heel of a hand.

Quin turned on a light. "She isn't moving in until next week. What is she doing here?"

An impossibly rhetorical question, Kiet thought: She is your mother, not mine. He did not reply, choosing instead to stare. Quin Canh, his first serious romantic interest since his wife Tien perished in the 1966 cholera epidemic, was a forty-three-year-old woman who looked even better naked than clothed. She was slim and supple. Black hair lightly traced with gray extended below her shoulders. Delicate lines radiated from her eyes. Tiny ripples of cellulite on the backs of her thighs excited him too and he didn't know exactly why. He just knew that she—the body and the being who was its caretaker—was marching into middle age with incredible grace and that he wanted to be along for the remainder of the trip. Bamsan Kiet was in love.

Quin returned his stare with a glare, silently telling him that an erection was an inappropriate response to this crisis. She put on a robe and said, "I saw her yesterday. They were getting along well enough."

The other part of the *they* was Quin's older sister, with whom Le had lived since the death last year of Quin's father, a produce vendor at the public market. He hadn't died, Kiet thought nastily; he had escaped.

Kiet got out of the mood and out of bed. He stretched, catching a glimpse in the dresser mirror of a man who did not look better naked than clothed. The wear and tear of half a century on the planet showed. He was large for a Luongan, nearly a head taller and too many kilograms heavier than his short, lean countrymen. He wore the husk of a Buddha, yet lacked the Gautama's inner serenity. The worst of both worlds, Quin believed. The twin killers of stress and flab. But she was working on it. The physical erosion. Ingrained attitudes and anxieties. Total renovation of the man she loved.

"What do you think happened?"

"My cretinous brother-in-law," Quin said. "What else?"

2

Quin loathed him. She could not bear to repeat his name. Although tension between Kiet and Le was thicker than Hickorn's humidity, fairness forced him to side with the old lady. Quin's sister's husband worked for the Golden Tiger Brewery and was exceedingly fond of his employer's product. He had the embittered alcoholic's flair for confrontation.

The noise on the door continued. "Maybe it isn't her," Kiet said hopefully.

"You know it is. I have to answer."

"If he struck her, I'll arrest him," Kiet said.

"He uses words, not fists, Bamsan. You know that. Whether you throw him in your jail or not, Mother is still moving in with me. She can't take it any longer."

Quin had the disconcerting ability to read his mind. Le's installation in Quin's apartment would eliminate their privacy, their wonderful routine. He had hoped for one more week of paradise.

"Go ahead," he said. "Yell through the door that you don't buy from door-to-door peddlers."

Quin smiled, pinched his midsection roll, and slipped out of his grasp. Kiet, now alone while his future happiness was being altered, slumped on the edge of the bed. If his potential mother-in-law was out there, he would have to make peace. Or at least try. No more procrastination.

Kiet and Quin had not vowed to wed, nor had they discussed the possibility. Marriage as a general topic was coming up frequently in conversation, though. Both parties spoke kindly of the institution, in carefully abstract terms. A critical step, Kiet knew. It was like diplomacy, where you played oblique word games until everybody was certain everybody else was of a mind. Then you proposed the trade agreement or whatever, hashed out the details, then sat down and signed. Kiet was thinking that if and when Quin and he put quill pens to parchment, the leathery antique in the hallway would be his dowry.

Her dislike of him was based on prejudice. Le Canh

despised policemen, with some justification. When dealing with the natives, the French colonial *Préfecture de Police* did not always remember that they were public servants. After independence, Luongan officers carried on as they had been trained. Kiet's highest priority upon appointment as superintendent was the eradication of brutality and corruption. He had been largely successful, but traditional ways lingered, and food merchants such as Le and her departed husband were succulent prey for petty extortionists.

Kiet was a policeman. A uniformed thug who fondled his nightstick while accepting a pineapple as a "gift" was a policeman. It did not count that the former had and would still eagerly fire and prosecute the latter. They were both *policemen*. They were therefore interchangeable, any member of the species being an unsuitable mate for her daughter.

His dislike of her was based on her prejudice, although the idea of a mother-in-law under his roof, any mother-in-law, was as repugnant as Le herself. Age was venerated in Luong and homes tended to be matriarchal. The grandmother pretty much ran the household. Kiet's own mother was deceased. She could not be installed as a counterbalance, to look after her son's domestic rights. Le's gloom and her resentments would set the tone. The environment would not be conducive to newlywed romance.

Then there was Bao Canh, Quin's son, the only offspring of a marriage that ended in divorce a decade before. Bao was not an immediate problem. He was a drummer in a rock-and-roll band that played in a Hickorn nightclub.

But if they joined as man and wife, the lad would be a significant problem. Kiet's every attempt to initiate conversation resulted in sullen grunts. Kiet admitted partial responsibility for the "communication breakdown" and "generation gap," psychological terminology passed on to him in sympathy by Captain Binh, his adjutant. Binh had lived in the United States for a year and knew of these things, which were North American epidemics.

Kiet, thus advised, had tried to "relate" by introducing as a topic his own enthusiasm for contemporary Western popular music. He was especially fond of Elvis Presley and Slim Whitman. Bao reacted with gleeful contempt. He had never heard of them and knew he would hate them if he had.

Bao's band was entitled Plutonium Gecko. Kiet had gone into their club once, a dive catering to college students called Mom's Café, and listened to what Binh had forewarned him as being a blend of punk and heavy metal. The quartet shrieked lyrics of death and forcible sex and nuclear holocaust. They sounded like tortured livestock. Alienation widened, Bao's grunting replies becoming almost inaudible, usually accompanied by smirks.

It was the boy's appearance too. Kiet could never be a friend, let alone a stepfather, unless Bao Canh again looked human. That hair. Kiet could not believe the hair. Bao shaved his head, reserving a longitudinal strip centered on his scalp. It was described by Captain Binh as Mohawk, although American native tribesmen who originated the style had not dyed theirs a vivid green.

Quin didn't care. Her son could do no wrong. She accused Kiet of being old-fashioned and resistant to change. Bao was creative, eagerly exploring individuality and self-expression; that his hair glowed in the dark was irrelevant. Their fiercest argument had erupted when Kiet challenged her tolerance, asking snidely if there was an extraterrestrial recessive gene in their family history. Martian ancestors, perhaps. Motherly protectiveness had battered him into submission. Kiet henceforth spoke of Bao Canh only when Quin Canh first spoke of Bao Canh to him.

Quin returned. "Bamsan, why aren't you dressed? And why are you shaking your head?"

"A crick in my neck," Kiet lied. He was actually shaking

5

his head in frustration, wondering why true love was so unfair to its victims.

"Bamsan, please, get dressed."

"It is as you thought?"

"That—that creature came home drunk again. Mother was sitting in his favorite chair, darning one of *his* stockings. He went wild, accusing her of forcing him out of his home. First my chair, he said. Next my bed. I won't repeat the names he called her. He has my sister so browbeaten that she can't stand up to him anymore."

Kiet sorted through his clothing—shorts and slacks and sandals and shirt, which Quin had collected and arranged neatly on the dresser. Kiet, in passion, stimulated by this woman as he had never been by any woman except Tien, was inclined to disrobe as if he were discarding live grenades. "Sad," he said. "A shame."

"Mother brought the belongings she could carry in a taxi. I'll go over tomorrow. Sister and I will pack for her while the beast is at his brewery. Will you please hurry!"

Kiet put on his shirt and said, "Stall her. I'll be presentable in a few minutes."

"Bamsan, you can't stay."

Kiet looked at her and thought he understood. "Oh. You in just your bathrobe. That might be obvious. Get some clothes on. She will never guess."

"No! We're by ourselves."

"Excuse me?"

Quin was facing the mirror, frantically brushing the evidence, the tangles of postcoital siesta out of her hair. "You and I, we are alone in my apartment."

Kiet said, "Are alone. Soon to be past tense. Were alone. Quin, I promise to smile and be courteous."

"Listen to me. We are unchaperoned."

Kiet looked at her mirror image and recalled another expression Binh had gleaned during his twelve months in America. "We are consenting adults," he said.

"Mother does not consent, Bamsan. She has never seen us together, just the two of us. It isn't proper."

"Unchaperoned," Kiet muttered.

She placed the hairbrush on the dresser top and sat on Kiet's lap. "I am still her little girl. I am unmarried, entertaining a gentleman guest without supervision. I would lose face and Mother would be even more distraught than she already is."

Kiet capitulated with a heavy sigh, patted her rump, and accepted a chaste kiss. Victory hers, Quin sprang to her feet and blew him another. "See me tomorrow?"

Kiet replied with a grunt and a nod. Quin ran to the front room and gave the old crone delaying excuses. Kiet ran to the rear door in the kitchen, buttoning and zippering. He descended a dark and rickety stairway, feeling like a sneaky, hormone-crazed adolescent fleeing an enraged father.

Love, he decided, was one horrendous mess.

2

Kiet's bicycle had not been stolen. In these times, its very presence, leaning against the wall of Quin's apartment building where he had left it, was noteworthy, an unpleasant surprise. Since the beginning of the opium war, crime had funneled into Kiet's beloved Hickorn as if the city were one large sewer main. Previously the Hickorn Police Department license badge dangling from the handlebars by leather thongs would have been an absolute deterrent. No longer. Criminals were practicing their trade at every level. Thievery and violence that seemed almost random was not. An addict would risk death to snatch Kiet's bicycle and barter it for a pipe of opium.

As no dope fiend had seized the opportunity and his bicycle, thereby affording him a valid excuse for hailing a taxicab and riding the two kilometers to his home, Kiet eased onto the seat and began pedaling. His regimen of fitness and robust health was recent. His butt was tender and the seat was as hard as stone. He came out of the alley and turned north on Rue Ho Chi Minh, thinking again of the lesser-of-two-evils cliché.

Binh had blown the engine of the department Citroën, the only automobile at his disposal. This left a choice between bicycle and motorbike. Kiet distrusted the stability of the sputtering scooters, and their exhaust fumes gave him headaches. The bicycle solved his transportation problem and it placated Quin, who had been nagging him into an exercise program.

Kiet paused at the corner, the Avenue Charles de Gaulle intersection, and massaged his aching buns. He was in no hurry and it would be foolish to overdo. Quin even said so. She was a certified nurse who taught her profession at Luong University's College of Medicine. It was with authority, then, that she had diagnosed Kiet as possessing a Westerner's cardiovascular system.

He drew in a deep breath, allowing his pulse to decelerate. No telling what might happen to a body so decayed by indulgence and neglect, how many chunks of cholesterol might break loose from the vast slabs within, he thought, poking the fun at her and himself that he would never dare orally.

He listened to the night. The immediate area, a neighborhood of apartment houses half a kilometer from the university, was quiet. Traffic was light. Most residents were indoors, sounds of habitation subdued by doors, walls, and imminent bedtime. Orderly and comforting.

But in the not-so-distance distance, toward downtown and the Strip, the noise of pleasure-seeking and mischief clung in the air like a foul vapor. Motor vehicle engines, motor vehicle horns, tinny music, shouts, peals of laughter. Kiet glanced at his watch: 9 P.M. Not orderly, not comforting, he mused, and until recently, decidedly abnormal for the hour. Captain Binh's peculiar American slang assertion that Hickorn's sidewalks "rolled up after dark" was obsolete.

The opium war again came to mind. Kiet could not obliterate it from his thoughts any more than he could from Hickorn's streets. To his knowledge, Luong's opium

10

war was the third. The first and most odious occurred in China in the 1840s. The British imported Indian opium to China and traded it for silver. When the Chinese objected to the habit imposed on its populace and destroyed opium stocks near Canton, the British attacked. Their subsequent victory and the Treaty of Nanking ceded Hong Kong to them and opened principal Chinese ports to other foreigners. That combination of brutal suppression and profit motive set the tenor for European colonialism in Asia.

Laos, in 1967, was the arena of the second. Golden Triangle poppy farmers sold their prolific harvests to two varieties of bandit warlords—the Shan United Army, a Burmese separatist faction allegedly dealing in opium to finance a political struggle against the Rangoon government, and the Kuomintang, remnants of Chiang Kai-shek's Nationalist Chinese Army that had been chased out of their homeland during the Communist takeover.

A Shan caravan loaded with sixteen tons of opium, heading south from Burma, sought to avoid paying customary taxes to the Kuomintang. The Chinese gave chase. Fierce battles ensued. Laotian warplanes joined in, dropping bombs on anything that moved. Royal Lao Army paratroopers fluttered down and grabbed the opium in the name of democracy, worldwide drug eradication, and half a million dollars' worth of narcotics their commanding general didn't have to pay for.

Compromises were soon struck and normalcy returned to the business. In the following quarter century, only the names of some prime players and the relative strengths of their forces changed. Everybody thrived. Interruptions to the peace came from outsiders, the armies of the Golden Triangle nations and Western drug enforcement teams. These forays ranged in success from serious setback to annoyance, too often the latter.

The third opium war, Kiet's nightmare, was (and is) quite similar to the second, the handiwork of chaos and greed. Between six months and a year earlier, the opium

11

hierarchies experienced a phenomenally high attrition rate. Bandit chieftains who didn't die of old age retired to villas and concubines. Younger men on the rise had ideas and ambitions. These ideas and ambitions included neither rivals inside their ranks nor the competition.

Gunfire was exchanged, friendships and alliances terminated. Territories were split by paramilitary force and divided again. Poppy-growing regions were occupied and defended like medieval fiefdoms. Burmese and Thai army units, encouraged by the discord, increased pressure on the trade. Agencies of prosperous heroin-consuming countries were delighted by the confusion and donated even more money, helicopters, and advice to the cause.

The free-for-all and the advantages taken by soldiers and lawmen because of it may have slowed the river of poison streaming into the veins of New York and Philadelphia and Montreal addicts as claimed—Kiet had read a magazine article that actually used this hydraulic metaphor—but he was unconvinced. From his perspective, the flow had not been plugged but rather diverted into a network of tributaries.

This network (Kiet's own metaphor) was his curse. The network was the Kingdom of Luong. The bickering and gunslinging and interdiction had disrupted regular trafficking circuits through Burma and Thailand. While Luong was by any definition a Golden Triangle nation along with Laos, Thailand, and Burma, and while some poppies were farmed in her northern highlands and remote western provinces, the bulk of the drug had been transported to its eventual markets from neighboring port cities. Luong was landlocked; until the opium war, it was not an attractive embarkation point.

At the moment, an estimated 50 percent of the Golden Triangle's opium gum and its end products, morphine base and heroin, moved through Luong. The narcotics traveled by jungle paths and rivers, by routes thought to be impassable, carried on hacked-out trails and malarial waterways by pioneers made intrepid by money. It also traveled conventionally, via air and established roads.

Drug enforcement experts believed Hickorn to be a major terminus. How the drug came in and how it subsequently went out, controlled by whom, remained a mystery. Although depressingly few arrests had been made and piddling quantities of the drug had been confiscated, Kiet accepted the drug wizards' analysis. He did not have to stumble on a mound of white powder to be convinced. It was so apparent. The human seepage now in his city had not been attracted by the climate.

Kiet sighed. The rest stop probably had not been beneficial to his cardiovascular mess. Not if you asked Quin. His cogitation over the opium war, the heavy thinking and anxiety and anger and bafflement, was flooding adrenaline and other injurious chemicals into his bloodstream. It was as bad as eating pork fat, she said. The stuff must be burned off before it bonds to already-narrowed coronary arteries.

Kiet pictured a malodorous goo pumping through him, depositing on his vessels a substance similar to undercoating sprayed on the belly of an automobile. The image was as fanciful as frightening, but one could not be too careful. Kiet started riding.

Upright, shifting weight from pedal to pedal, gathering speed, he felt his slipstream. Velocity cooled the warm, moist air and evaporated his perspiration. He felt good. Three blocks northward, at Avenue Leonid Brezhnev, the chain came off its sprocket. A tiring Kiet dismounted and reattached it.

He was due for another break anyhow. His legs were getting rubbery and he was swallowing oxygen in great gulps. He ran a hand across his stomach, amazed at the decrease in volume. Surely this reduction in flab should be rewarded. *Would* be rewarded.

The sole benefit of the opium war had been the proliferation of imported luxury goods, sponges to sop all that excess money. Among them were frozen American desserts. The minuscule freezer compartment in Kiet's refrigerator had room to store one pastry baked by Sara Lee or Mrs. Smith. He did not remember which lady's splendid recipe was in there, but he did remember that it was chocolate, smothered in whipped cream, garnished with chocolate shavings.

Quin would rip out his hair if she learned, but lovers should be entitled to innocent secrets, shouldn't they? It was not a case of infidelity or even impure thoughts. Kiet lusted after Sara in her kitchen, not in her bedroom.

A kilometer and a half to home. Kiet was going to eat the entire luscious thing. He would do so with a spotless conscience—the caloric intake could not possibly exceed calories burned by this grueling ride.

Kiet lifted a leg over the bicycle and noticed a strange lull. For five or six seconds he heard only a gentle breeze that rustled leaves of the tamarind trees lining Rue Ho Chi Minh. Then he heard a gunshot. It was a big bang, an elephant rifle or a shotgun. He heard screams. The gunshot and the screams came from the west, from the direction of the Strip.

Kiet groaned, stood on a pedal, and leaned westward. There would be no rendezvous with Lady Sara this evening.

14

3

In a past time so faraway and tranquil that Kiet thought of it as a bygone era, there was no Strip. This was before the opium war, before the introduction of television to Luong. Kiet knew that his nostalgia was for a false past. The faraway "era" had ended scarcely more than a year ago, and from his vantage point as superintendent of police, Hickorn had never been especially tranquil. But because of present circumstances he could not rid himself of the notion.

The street whose four northernmost blocks composed the Strip was, in the mid-1970s, designated Rue Pol Pot by Prince Novisad Pakse. Kiet remembered well how His Royal Highness loathed this exigency of Luongan neutralist politics, how geography and military weakness compelled him to honor a monster. Shortly thereafter Vietnam invaded Cambodia, displacing the Khmer Rouge and their genocidal commander as the regional menace. Pol Pot and his followers became guerrillas, fighting a hit-and-run war against the Vietnamese that was reminiscent of North Vietnam versus America not very many years prior.

15

His Royal Highness left Rue Pol Pot as is. The irony of Pot's reduced position was not lost on him, nor was the possibility of a Khmer Rouge comeback. He mostly lost interest. It was and always had been a minor north–south side street that intersected at a needle's point with Ma San Boulevard, a stretch of pavement too lightly traveled by foreigners for its designation to be damagingly offensive.

Television, not politics, was finally responsible for Pol Pot's banishment. One black-and-white station transmitted in Hickorn. Kiet loved their fare of American frontier dramas, but His Royal Highness's interest in the medium developed far beyond *The Cisco Kid* and *Gunsmoke*, and coincided with his abiding passion—pocket billiards.

The unsightly dish-shaped antenna affixed atop the Royal Palace's east wing and a full-color, forty-five-inch receiver brought the outside world to Prince Pakse's private parlor. Among the signals shooting downward from space satellites were those originating at a sporting event network in the American province of Connecticut. This station, named the Entertainment and Sports Programming Network, utilizing technological magic that Kiet would never attempt to comprehend, included billiards competitions in its vast athletic repertoire. The day after viewing a nine-ball tournament, which he preserved for future enjoyment on a videotape recording device, Prince Pakse consigned Rue Pol Pot to history.

Kiet rode to the western tip of Avenue Leonid Brezhnev. He propped his bicycle on a fire hydrant and tried to postpone reality by gazing at the silky mist hovering over the Ma San River. He tried to block out the commotion, tried to visualize Rue ESPN when it was a quiet street of shops and eateries, before His Royal Highness's tribute to Connecticut billiards broadcasters disappeared from parlance. Before every Hickorn taxi and pedicab driver in town hawked Rue ESPN as the Strip to their passengers, promising with unfortunate candor that anything could be bought or sold, that any appetite could be slaked.

The Hong Kong Bar, the Princess Snack Bar, Monica's, Double Happiness, Four Oceans, Kontiki Klub, the Moulin Rouge, the Green Latrine, the Watusi, Triple Ripple, Colette's, Madame Olga's, Bimbos Are We, Mom's Café. Kiet pictured those sex and drink and narcotics parlors without seeing them. He had visited them often enough in the line of duty.

The worst of the execrable lot was the Scarlet Mongoose, a triangular structure whose shape was the needle's point at the confluence of Ma San Boulevard, Avenue Leonid Brezhnev, and Rue ESPN. Its proprietor was an American mobster and the commotion of onlookers and police officers was coming from there, clustering around a bright-red automobile that was parked at a peculiar angle, partially on the sidewalk, its nose facing the Scarlet Mongoose entrance. Kiet heard his name called.

Captain Binh ran to him and said breathlessly, "Superintendent, how did you receive the report so fast? I'm the night desk officer and I didn't see you at headquarters."

Kiet sighed. "Attribute me to splendid luck. My evening is overflowing with it."

"Superintendent, what's the matter with your shirt?"

Kiet looked at his handsome, bright-eyed adjutant, who was invariably immaculate in starched whites, spit-polished shoes, and three gold captain's pips gleaming on shoulder boards. Binh disapproved of Kiet's informal and sometimes rumpled apparel, but his disapproval was usually and wisely expressed only by the tilt of his eyebrows. I must have violated an inexcusable law of fashion, Kiet thought. He looked down and saw that he had. His shirt was bunched. In his haste to dress at Quin's, he had buttoned buttons into the wrong buttonholes.

"Never mind," he said, making corrections. "What do we have?"

"A murder," Binh said. "A gangland-style slaying."

Binh studied law enforcement science for a year in America at their District of Columbia police constabulary.

The young adjutant returned home brimming with innovations that seldom applied to Hickorn and with an irritating wealth of United States cop slang. The idiom spoke by their organized criminals and by those devoted to jailing them included, yes, *gangland-style slaying*.

"Ah," Kiet said. "Hands tied behind him. In the trunk of that red automobile. A bullet to the back of the head."

"Uh-uh," Binh said. "If you're going to whack somebody out just to get rid of him, you order that kind of contract hit."

"Certainly," Kiet agreed.

"But if you want to set an example, you go for pizzazz."

"Of course."

"You blow him away for everybody to see."

"I heard a loud gunshot," Kiet said.

"We don't have the perp or his weapon, but five'll get you ten it was a sawed-off shotgun. I'm guessing a hand-loaded dumdum round. Twelve gauge. Heavy artillery."

Perp? Kiet remembered. Perpetrator. "Witnesses?"

Binh smirked and shook his head. "Witnesses on the Strip, Superintendent? That'll be the day."

"Who is the victim?"

"We don't know. There's no ID on him and he's hamburger from the neck up. C'mon, I'll give you the grand tour."

Kiet followed his second-in-command to the scene. He was not eager to see what he had to see. His deepest secret was his aversion to blood and gore. That Hickorn's ranking police official fell uncontrollably nauseous at the sight of human violence was unthinkable. To lose the healthful and marginably palatable vegetarian dinner Quin had fed him would cause an irrevocable loss of face.

Binh pointed to the automobile, a convertible. The driver's door was open and the presumed driver was curled in a question-mark position on the street. Kiet locked his eyes on the vehicle, which was being searched by two uniformed officers.

18

"Looks to me like he saw what was coming down and decided to drive around the perp. Then he realized he was cut off and tried to bug out on foot," Binh said. "He didn't have a prayer. They zotzed him before he ran three steps."

Zotzed, Kiet thought. Whacked out. He forced himself to look at the corpse. Thankfully, there was a blood-drenched rag covering what remained of the head. Another officer was bent over, chalking the pavement surrounding the victim. Why did Binh insist on this procedure? Kiet again wondered. He had asked him once and Binh had said that this was the way it was done.

"It had to be opium," Binh continued. "He has to have burned some biggie on a drug deal."

"No argument there," Kiet said. "Where is Little Big Vinnie?"

"Inside his club. He's got a knack of being close to the action, doesn't he, Superintendent?"

Vincent "Little Big Vinnie" Jones owned the Scarlet Mongoose. He indeed seemed to be on the periphery of the Strip's rowdyism and mayhem, though never at the center where he could be yanked out by the neck and thrown into jail (Kiet's favorite nonsexual fantasy) to languish until the next century.

"Have you interviewed Mr. Jones?"

"No, not really." Binh said. "He told me that the music accompanying his floor show was so loud he didn't hear anything. I was holding off anyhow, until I saw you."

"In that respect Mr. Jones is believable," Kiet said, listening to discordant guitar twangs and drumrolls pulsing through the doorway. "Shall we?"

"Yeah, I suppose," Binh said, walking in. "Sounds like the feature act is concluding. If you ask me, Superintendent, Little Big Vinnie gives sex a bad name."

No argument there either. As Kiet entered, he glanced at Little Big Vinnie's facsimile of a marquee, a sandwich-board sign sided by a porky bouncer who recognized Hickorn's number-one and number-two policemen. The neckless cretin grinned obsequiously and swept an arm toward the gaiety, saying "No cover charge for you gentlemen. No sir, bwana-san."

The poster on the sign was a full-length photograph of the Scarlet Mongoose's headline performer, a redheaded Australian stripteaser in pasties and a G-string who at six feet tall had an Amazon's figure and a face that Kiet regarded as exquisitely homely even for a Caucasian. The caption advertised TESS TWITCH, The Down Under Wunder and her SEXsational Down Under.

The smoke of cigarette tobacco and other vegetable matter was already making Kiet's eyes water. Lights had been extinguished but for a spotlight trained on the stage. With a wrist flick, Tess Twitch shed a G-string, her last garment. She dangled it tantalizingly on a toe and volleyed it into the cheering audience.

The band stopped playing. Tess Twitch raised her arms, amplifying the applause. Her smile was so wide and unchanging that Kiet wondered if she suffered a disorder of the facial nerves. She held her nose and hopped off the raised stage, a nymph splashing daintily into a wading pool. The spotlight beam stuck to her like an appendage. Everyone clapped and howled.

Tess bent at the knees, an obscene curtsy. It was a cue. A sizable portion of the patrons, Westerners and Japanese and Singapore Chinese and Thai, visiting businessmen of some ilk, and Luongans with plenty of money to spend, came out of their chairs. They hit the floor as if an air raid siren had sounded, utterly oblivious to the filth grinding into their polyester slacks and Hawaiian shirts.

Tess walked among the inflamed multitude, gathering one after another the 5,000-zin notes they had folded lengthwise and placed on their noses. She was squatting and plucking the equivalent of seven U.S. dollars with her pudenda. Each retrieval was recorded by a cymbal clash.

"Sexsational down under," Kiet muttered, surveying the room.

"You'd have to be hornier than a three-peckered goat," Binh said, shaking his head. "I wouldn't touch her with a ten-foot pole."

"Where is he?"

"Right on the fifty-yard line."

"Excuse me?"

"Front and center. There. That table pushed up to the stage. He keeps tabs on his merchandise. If a customer plays grab-ass, he sics his goons on them. Any woman headlining for Vinnie, he's banging her. They're his personal property."

Vincent Jones was leaning back in a chair, his snakeskin boots resting on the two other chairs at the table. He wore tight black slacks, a red suede dinner jacket, and a ruffled white silk shirt. The top half of the shirt was undone. Gold chains nested in a thicket of black chest hair. The diamond set in the ring on his left little finger was impressive. This "pinkie ring" had verified to Captain Binh his reputed membership in a Cleveland, Ohio province, U.S. of A. crime family. "Button men," "made guys," affected pinkie rings, Binh advised.

Binh's research had also revealed the origin of his Little Big Vinnie sobriquet. Jones was a short, thin, and swarthy white man in his mid-thirties. His narrow face and beady eyes reminded Kiet of a craven parrot. He had been born small and never caught up. In the fourth grade of grammar school, three years before his formal education ended, tired of being bullied by larger children, Jones nicknamed himself Big Vinnie. To make it stick, with the moral and financial support of his father and uncles who believed that money and terror rightfully accomplished anything, he hired sixth-graders to beat up his tormentors. Jones learned a valuable lesson and carried this credo into adult life, but when his growth ceased—shoulder high to Kiet—the "Little" modifier was inevitable.

Vincent Jones acknowledged the policemen with a curt nod. They were standing between him and Tess Twitch,

21

and Jones canted his head to see around the obstruction. His lips were moving, so Kiet assumed he was counting her gynecological receipts.

Kiet accepted Jones's cordial invitation to join his table by jerking back the free chairs. Reptile-skin boots clunked on the grimy floor. Little Big Vinnie reached skyward, beseeching the patron saints of justice, saying "What the fuck now, Kiet? What did I do?"

Kiet fastidiously brushed off the chairs before he and Binh sat. "How could she embezzle you?" he said. "Where would she hide it?"

"Tess? These broads, they got no loyalty. You look, Kiet. She got them bills in her hands and she's waving 'em around. She could palm 'em to some gink and they'd divvy the proceeds later. You're not on top of things, they rob you blind."

"*Little* Big Vinnie. The rotten pussy king," Binh said, shaking his head in disgust. "What a guy."

Jones laughed and pointed at Binh. "Your boyo here, Kiet, he don't shave twice a week and he's telling me what's good quiff and what ain't. Lemme dig out a five-thou zin bill for boyo. He hits the deck for Tess, it's the closest he ever been to heaven."

Kiet gripped Binh's forearm, restraining him. When the lad was morally outraged, he became feisty and Jones knew it. The gangster's gibe at Binh's sexual experience was inaccurate—he was an eligible young bachelor and accomplished deflowerer—and Jones knew that too. A diversion, a changing of the subject, a brouhaha over insulted manhood, was Jones's aim. No, thank you, thought Kiet.

"A man was killed outside your establishment," he said.

"Outside, pally. *Outside*," Jones said. "You said it. You wanna blame me for goofball street crime, you're way outta line. I'm a respectable businessman. You hassle me because you got a cowboy-and-Indian number going in this hick town of yours, you're a million miles off the mark.

22

I broke any laws? I been under arrest lately? I ain't budged for two hours and fifty witnesses will swear to it. Guy comes in and says a guy got wasted, I'm the one who says for him to go call the cops. I'm a public-spirited citizen."

"We suspect opium as the motive," Kiet said.

Up once more went Little Big Vinnie's justice-beseeching arms. "Opium? What do I know from opium?"

"Why else are you in Hickorn, Mr. Jones?"

"I'm not saying shit don't exist, Kiet. I'm not even saying that I didn't hang out my shingle in your burg because of the extra bread circulating on account of it. All I *am* saying is that I'm a simple innkeeper. I sell food, drink, and entertainment. Guy gets scragged outside my place, *outside*, I'm as pissed as you are. It scares off business, but it's just one of them things. A coincidence."

Wasted. Scragged. Additional homicide euphemisms for Kiet's mobster slang file. And, of course, the declaration of coincidence. This public-spirited citizen, this simple inn-keeper, was the everlasting dupe of coincidences and police persecution. Kiet did not doubt that Little Big Vinnie could produce fifty sworn alibis, all thoughtfully providing typed and notarized statements. Kiet had expected no breakthrough clue, no slip of the tongue, no confession. This conversation with the thug was the same as the rest, circular and scatological, but he had to make the effort.

Kiet was spared further futility. A uniformed officer, one of the pair searching the car, came to the table and whispered in Binh's ear. His eyes widened. He said, "Superintendent, we're needed outside."

Little Big Vinnie laughed. "Outside. I told you that's where you should be playing cops and robbers. Don't let the door hit you in the ass, boys."

Kiet tugged on the furious Binh's arm, saying "No. Our day with Mr. Jones will come."

They went into the street and saw that seats and interior trim panels had been removed from the red convertible.

The dismantling was done without apparent damage, Kiet observed, presumably on the orders of Binh, an automotive enthusiast.

"I told them not to trash it," Binh said in confirmation. "This is a cherry set of wheels and it's impounded department property."

The second officer handed Binh a brick-size package that was wrapped in heavy paper and twine.

"They found it tied under the passenger seat springs, Superintendent," Binh said as he cut the twine with a pocketknife.

He exposed an approximate kilogram of white powder sealed in transparent plastic. Stamped on the plastic was LUONG WHITE NO. 1. Kiet groaned.

"*Luong* white!" Binh said, stunned.

"We had suspicions," Kiet said.

"Now we know, Superintendent. Opium isn't just being trafficked through Luong. We've got laboratories right here refining opium to heroin."

"Continue the murder investigation," Kiet said wearily. "Perhaps we shall be lucky."

"I'll put every available officer on canvassing duty," Binh said. "As you say, we might get lucky."

"I'm optimistic," Kiet lied. "We'll review what we have tomorrow."

Kiet trudged to his bicycle. It was gone. He was not surprised.

4

Early the following morning, 10 A.M. sharp, Kiet arrived at the Ministry of Defense. By this time, tea would have been sipped, breakfast pastries munched, malicious gossip updated. Federal functionaries would be commencing a day of writing interoffice memoranda, approving and disapproving and rerouting same, and confirming luncheon reservations with superiors they sought to befriend or with subordinates whose aspirations they feared. "Power lunches," according to Binh.

Although independence had been won thirty-five years ago, the Kingdom of Luong was steeped in a mandarin bureaucracy that would not go away. Kiet dearly wished it would. He hated officious clerks. He hated inertia.

Because his bicycle was an HPD crime statistic, he came by taxi. He got out, paid the driver, stretched, and inhaled perfumed air. Quin had recommended flower sniffing. Pausing to smell the flowers, to quote her. Supposedly the practice benefited one's cardiovascular mechanism.

But Quin's recommendation was vague. She had not advocated the aromatic compounds of any particular flower species as a superior dissolver of cholesterol. Kiet had not pursued an explanation. He knew his health-conscious lover. The explanation would have certainly overlapped into elevated blood pressure and alcohol consumption and who knows what else? He suspected that she was speaking figuratively.

Kiet inhaled literally, enjoying the fragrance of Mu Savhana, known for the rainbow of perennial blooms in its wide median as the Street of Flowers. The National Bank, National Assembly, every important ministry, and the Royal Palace were located on Mu Savhana. As far as he was concerned, despite never having traveled beyond Luong's borders, Mu Savhana was the most beautiful thoroughfare in the world.

It had but one blemish, the building he was about to enter. The Ministry of Defense was France's last Hickorn edifice, a monstrously ugly, three-story stucco cube decorated with upswept pagodalike overhangs, an architectural compromise to the natives by colonists who finally realized that they were governing Hickorn, not Paris. The French were constructing a trade pavilion, but Independence interrupted its completion. An infant military bureaucracy in need of space rapidly moved in. To this day, cornices were missing, window sashes were devoid of trimwork.

Kiet entered, carrying a paper bag that did not contain his lunch, power or otherwise. He hesitated and looked into a bay of desks, cubicles, and offices. Ceiling fans, lazing through their revolutions, seemed to set the work tempo. Black tie/white shirt civilians and khaki-clad military men, clerks one and all, studied documents with a practiced languor. Each desk had a tree of rubber stamps—stultifying instruments of official clout. An invading force that destroys our stamp-pad ink supply has an easy conquest, Kiet thought with a sigh. He climbed stairs to Minister of Defense Cuong Van's top-floor office suite.

The minister's aide-de-camp, a frazzled army major, ushered Kiet into Van's inner office as if he had been expected. It looked like moving day. Carpeting had been pulled up, fixtures and cabinets dismantled. Van's desk was in pieces. Kiet found him in a corner, working from a chair and using an overturned wastebasket as a temporary desk.

"Bosha, you're amazingly punctual."

Cuong Van and Bamsan Kiet were lifelong friends and *lycée* classmates. Van was one of very few who addressed Kiet by his childhood diminutive; "bosha" was colloquial Luongan for runt, and Kiet had been one until an adolescent growth spurt shot him above his peers. "Excuse me?"

"I dispatched a messenger to your headquarters barely ten minutes ago. I've got a problem that requires your help, Bosha. You brought your lunch?"

Kiet held up the paper bag. "No, Cuong. I left headquarters before the messenger arrived. I have a problem that requires *your* help and this is it. Please, yours first?"

Cuong Van stood. Short and wiry, he wore glasses as thick as his hair was thin. His body hadn't deviated a kilogram in weight or a degree of muscle tone since he starred as a striker on the Luongan national soccer team. Kiet credited some of Van's success to underestimation. Political and military opponents of today were caught as flat-footed as the Pakistani and Cambodian fullbacks he had streaked past in the 1950s.

Prior to his appointment to this post, Van had served as commander in chief of the Royal Luongan Army. Kiet had been delighted by the promotion. A first cousin of His Royal Highness, Cuong Van was loyal, competent, and scrupulously honest. He had extinguished numerous coup d'état plots before they caught fire, several with Kiet's aid.

Van reached into a pocket and handed Kiet two small black objects. "Look at these, Bosha."

One was circular, the other rectangular. Neither was larger than a throat lozenge. "Electrical components?"

27

"Yes. Bugs."

"Bugs?"

"Miniature transmitters."

"Ah, bugs. Miniature electronic voyeurs. Where did you locate them, Cuong?"

"We found the button inside my telephone mouthpiece. The square bug was glued to a drapery bracket. Lately there's been a rash of clairvoyance. People know decisions I make before orders are cut."

"Specific areas of telepathy?"

"Specifically the opium war situation, Bosha. It's no secret that the Second Military District has perpetually dabbled in the trade. Regardless of who I assigned to key command slots, they were seduced by the money. I've been shuffling senior officers back and forth to impede empire building. Plans for opium incursions originate with my staff and myself. Of late, everything is common knowledge before it happens. Lon Muoi has a technical background. I had him sweep the office. Muoi mined these little gems."

Kiet nodded knowingly. The Second Military District in the northern highlands, based at Obon, had a twofold duty. To resist Communist Luong Rouge guerrillas by pinpointing their strongholds and attacking them. To guard Luong's northern frontier, the Golden Triangle overlap, and to harass encroaching Kuomintang and Shan opium caravans.

Government efforts contradicted the mission. Raids were as often as not accidental, self-preservation skirmishes fought by timid patrols that blundered into confrontations. Results were usually inconclusive and occasionally disastrous, although every gory outcome was reported as a smashing victory against monolithic communism and/or the international drug conspiracy. Royal Luongan troops had no heart for casualties in the name of any cause, especially when combat interfered with business.

"Who might have installed the bugs?" Kiet asked.

Cuong Van shrugged. "Anybody. My office is a busy place, and Muoi informed me that a person with superficial training and five minutes' privacy could have planted them. Is there a black market for eavesdropping paraphernalia you're aware of, Bosha, a common source?"

"Not to my knowledge, but I will look into it. Snooping is a favorite game of Luong's superpower guests, you know."

"I understand what you are insinuating. I surely do," Van said. "The Americans and Soviets share a zeal for spying on us and one another. I often think that they love espionage for the sheer sport of it, the professional challenge, whether the stakes are important or not."

"Opium has become as political as commercial," Kiet said. "Thus an even greater incentive for mischief."

"You investigate the streets, I'll investigate my ministry. One of us might stumble on a clue."

"Do you suspect disloyalty in your staff, Cuong? Any particular person?"

Van shook his head no and cocked a thumb downward. "You see what goes on in my paper factory. A Hickorn ministry appointment is what the Americans call the gravy train. I wish I could change the system. I can't. A document and a rubber stamp is power, food for the ego, but not food for the belly. Salaries are low. I can't eliminate as a suspect one solitary person who has access to this office."

"Money versus loyalty," Kiet said.

"You summarized the problem. An envelope bulging with zin for a five-minute risk."

"Indeed."

"Now your problem, Bosha. It's your turn," Van said, pointing at the paper sack.

Kiet removed the kilogram (one kilo exactly, per a weighing on headquarters' scale) package of Luong White No. 1, gave it to Cuong Van, and narrated the events pertinent to its acquisition.

29

"Pure heroin?"

"We estimate eighty to ninety percent purity."

"I didn't know you had a forensic laboratory."

"We don't. Nowadays my jail plays grudging host to growing numbers of addicts in the throes of withdrawal. They are not what we used to see, the wretched old men who smoked too many pipes in opium dens. They are younger people enslaved by the refined product. They are smokers and intravenous users. We aren't equipped to treat their agony, although my friend tells me that the Luong University College of Medicine is contemplating such a program.

"We tested this contraband on a guest who burgled homes to support his habit. We invited him to inhale a tiny quantity of the powder. 'Snorting' is the proper vernacular. He immediately relaxed and smiled blissfully."

"An effective test. And wonderfully barbaric," Van teased. "Our benefactors would be horrified."

Kiet smiled and said, "I do not expect criticism from outsiders. To cite that dreadful neologism, Luong is a Third World nation. We natives are therefore primitive. We know not what we do."

"The Mafia gangster, Jones. Can you implicate him in the heroin or the murder?"

"We shall concentrate on the murder. As you know, Cuong, thanks to bribes paid the National Assembly, the Hickorn Ordinance Book is being subtly revised. Prostitution and gambling have been relegated to the status of so-called victimless crimes, misdemeanors adjudicated by magistrates with a light fine. Since opium is responsible for the burgeoning number of 'victimless' victims, I predict a softening of narcotics laws too."

"As do I. And how is Quin, your university friend?"

Kiet blushed. "Splendidly splendid."

Van laughed. "She is too good for you, Bosha."

"She is indeed."

"Well, while it is again nice to chat with you, we aren't

30

accomplishing much. I am also dismayed by your evidence that heroin is now manufactured in Luong. How can I relieve your burden?"

"I'm presuming that the laboratories are in the highlands, close to the opium's points of entry."

"Increased pressure on the opium bandits?"

"Please."

Van juggled the bugs. "With these removed, I can and I will. Today is an anniversary, by the way. Zhu's fighter planes have had the Obon highway open for one month."

Kiet pondered that dubious enterprise. Air Vice-Marshal Souvang Zhu, commander of the Royal Luongan Air Force, was overflying Highway One, the 175-kilometer Hickorn–Obon highway, in ancient but nonetheless lethal fighter planes. Previously, road travel was extremely dangerous, and restricted to armed convoys. Bandit gangs and the pesky Luong Rouge sniped at or ambushed soldiers and civilians foolish enough to attempt the trip without adequate security. The theory behind the highway clearing was that the army could dispatch antiguerrilla squads, small-force drug eradication teams, Western advisers, and journalists to the highlands instantly, without elaborate preparations.

Kiet knew the theory was nonsense. So did Cuong Van. While the Kingdom of Luong might be comparatively backward, it was no stranger to the miracle of manned flight. The law of gravity did not prohibit one from loading supplies and elite personnel onto aircraft. Free passage between Luong's two major cities was a propaganda coup for the West, a demonstration of advancement against the Rouge and banditry, yes, but it multiplied opium-smuggling possibilities. Between Hickorn International Airport customs inspectors who were not hopelessly venal and Kiet's police officers, there were sufficient people to ransack every flying machine that touched down from Obon. A blockade of the automobiles, trucks, and motorbikes that gushed into the capital was not feasible. Not

31

with the manpower at his disposal. Van would contribute soldiers if Kiet asked. Kiet would not ask, absolutely not. The army complement required—legions of troopers searching vehicles and citizens—would give Hickorn an ambience of martial law. No, thank you.

Van inserted Air Vice-Marshal Zhu and his air cover into the discussion because the subject could not be avoided indefinitely. His friend Bosha had asked for a remedy, and Zhu's aerial swashbuckling was deemed by many to be a solution to Luong's woes, a magic pill. Zhu had gone over Van's head to sell his idiotic, self-serving scheme. To spare Van additional loss of face, Kiet deflected the subject.

"Foreign narcotics enforcement agents work through your ministry, Cuong. Are they making progress?"

"I apologize, Bosha, but politics renders a straight answer an impossibility. Upbeat news copy at home takes precedence. If the Americans burn a poppy field, they remind the wire services that the Soviets have not burned a poppy field all week, wondering loudly why not. Is there an insidious reason why the Russians are dragging their feet? And vice versa. Luckily for me, the opium war philosophies of Americans and Soviets are different. They're approaching the problem separately. Bickering is reduced and because it is, you are visiting me here today, rather than in a lunatic asylum."

"A scorched poppy farm is a scorched poppy farm," Kiet said, confused.

"I apologize further for not keeping you abreast. Our benefactors are intensifying their aid at a hot pace. Poppy eradication is a bad example. That is about the only action that conforms to both policies."

"Excuse me? *Both* policies?"

Van explained, "The Soviets are backing away from military support. They're leaving field engagement to the Americans. Mother Russia has a pugnacious image in our part of the world, and they'd like to dab cosmetics on the warts."

"Vietnam," Kiet said. "Support of Vietnamese aggression."

"Exactly. The Union of Soviet Socialist Republics is stressing alternative cropping. They've brought in a Cuban tropical agriculture specialist to counsel the peasants. Opium is out. Coffee, corn, and beans are in."

"Luong's opium production is a fraction of Burma's and Laos's. A few thousand hectares of Luongan coffee plants is preferable to none, but—"

"Right, Bosha. Window dressing. I know."

"The Americans?"

"No change."

"Ah," Kiet said. "Aircraft, guns, two-way radios, laser beams, satellite surveillance, computer printouts."

Van grinned. "Behave yourself. They're sincere."

"Tip Taylor," Kiet said, rolling his eyes, referring to Tyler Polk (Tip) Taylor, the senior drug enforcement adviser attached to the U.S. Embassy. Taylor was the son-in-law of Ambassador Smithson, the American ambassador. Kiet thought cynically that they could be biological father and son, their fanatical anticommunism a genetic trait.

Cuong Van said, "Bosha. Don't. I know your opinion of Sonny and Dad-in-law. They are ours to cherish and to cooperate with, and there is not a damn thing we can do about it."

There was a knock on the door. Van said come in. Associate Deputy Minister of Defense for Drug Enforcement Investigation Lon Muoi entered and said, "Sir, I was told that Superintendent Kiet was here. I thought you may require me to brief him."

Kiet and Muoi exchanged nods. No attempt was made to disguise a mutual animosity. Muoi was a twenty-six-year-old child with lazy eyes and an upturned nose that suggested haughtiness, an instance, Kiet thought, of the face as viewfinder to the soul. He was the dilettante son of a wealthy Hickorn rice wholesaler and processor. The father was an infinitely indulgent parent who sent the lad abroad at much expense to study whichever profession met his fancy at a given moment. Muoi would then return home and fail.

His airline pilot career terminated on his maiden flight—actually a nonflight—when he groundlooped one of Royal Air Luong's DC-3s, damaging it beyond repair, wiping out a third of their fleet. Next was computer electronics, but that succumbed stillborn, aborted by an indifference to mathematics. He was most recently a graduate of some Western drug agency academy, a propagandized and overstimulated operative against "the tears of the poppy," a commie-hating idolater of Tip Taylor and Souvang Zhu.

It wasn't Lon Muoi's abilities, or lack thereof, that failed him. His enthusiasm was his downfall. He was immature, flighty. Interest waned with the onset of pressure and hard work.

Muoi, like Air Vice-Marshal Zhu's highway-clearing silliness, was an unwanted addition to Van's Ministry of Defense. His job and flatulent title had been legislated by the National Assembly, a purchase made by his father. Kiet wondered how long he would last. So did Cuong Van.

"Thank you, but Minister Van has briefed me adequately," Kiet said coolly.

"We are thankful for your electronics expertise, Lon," Van said to ease the tension.

"One question, please," Kiet said. "How long did it take you to locate the bugs?"

"Fifteen minutes," Muoi said smugly.

"Speedy," Kiet said. "You are a veritable wizard."

Muoi looked at Kiet.

Van said, "Once more, Lon, thank you. Superintendent Kiet and I are grateful. Is there anything else?"

Muoi shook his head no and left.

"Bosha, you hurt his feelings," Van said in mock annoyance. "Go easy, will you? I have to get along with the boy."

"Sorry."

"Besides the obvious, what bothers you about him?"

Kiet got up. "I don't know."

"But you will tell me when you figure it out, won't you?"

"Yes," Kiet said. "Oh, yes."

5

The address of Hickorn Police Department Headquarters was 900 Alexandre Loubet. The street immortalized a nineteenth-century priest who had taken time from saving pagan souls to romanize the Luongan language. The French named the street long before Kiet's birth, and Prince Pakse had never tampered with the designation. His subjects were evenly split between Buddhist and Roman Catholic, and religious dialogue had not always been peaceful. An undercurrent existed that His Royal Highness wisely did not agitate.

The headquarters building was a blockhouse of tan stucco and massive timbers that had been a pre-Independence barracks and command center for legionnaires. The interior was Spartan and cold, little changed from the days of French hegemony. Boots echoed on hallway tile and the rooms reeked of musty permanence. Kiet liked the haunting austerity, the businesslike message it conveyed to police officers and unwilling guests alike.

Cuong Van's aide-de-camp drove Kiet there in a Jeep. He went through the gate and saw in the courtyard his

Citroën, which had been undergoing repair since Captain Binh exploded the engine. Kiet knew too well Binh's maniacal driving habits and had never completely swallowed his mechanical gibberish, his ridicule of French automotive engineering, his assignment of blame to crankshaft metal fatigue. More likely, Binh had attempted to break the sound barrier in second gear.

He stopped behind the car. Something was wrong with its low-slung streamlined shape. The rear end was too high and the front almost touched the ground. Abnormally wide tires encircled aluminum alloy wheels. The Citroën seemed to be crouching, as if to pounce. He walked closer and saw riveted to the hood panel a boxlike sheet-metal protuberance.

Kiet groaned and trudged inside on legs weighted by yet another bad surprise. He said nothing to anybody and went straight to his office. Captain Binh spotted Kiet and followed him in.

"Well," Binh said, beaming. "How do you like it?"

Kiet felt obliged by Binh's giddiness to advance the conversation in small increments. Each explanatory morsel must be savored. "The Citroën?"

"Yeah. What do you think, Superintendent?"

"It is fully repaired?"

"Is it! Like you wouldn't believe."

"I notice some, uh, modifications."

"Well, since it was already out of commission, I figured it would be smart to upgrade. That car was a dog, Superintendent."

"Excuse me?"

"A gutless wonder. It couldn't get out of its own way."

"You are telling me that power has been added to the motor?"

Binh cleared his throat and picked at his fingernails. "Well, you're kind of restricted by the stock engine. It's just a four-banger, you know. You could mill the heads and go to dual carbs, but top-end torque would still be a joke."

38

"You are saying that you substituted motors?"

"The garage that the department contracts to lucked into a Chevy Three-fifty, Superintendent. Some guy totaled out a Caprice Classic and they bought the salvage. The body's history but the engine was undamaged. Less than thirty thousand miles on it."

"A Chevy? That is an American-made Chevrolet, a gigantic sedan?"

"Yeah, a land yacht, a gunboat. The head mechanic at the garage is a genius, Superintendent. He stiffened the frame and shoehorned the Three-fifty in, no sweat."

"A substantially larger motor, then?"

"A V-eight has twice as many cylinders as a four. Our rig will do eighty without breathing hard."

"Eighty kilometers per hour?"

"Uh-uh. *Miles.* Scumbag dope dealers can afford hot cars, Superintendent. The red convertible last night, you know. We need a vehicle that can't be outrun. The Citroën'll blow the doors off anything in town."

The capability to detonate a criminal's car doors? Kiet did not pursue that bizarre piece of slang; no, thank you. He instead shut his eyes and converted eighty miles per hour into kilometers. One twenty-five, one thirty. He visualized motorized pursuit of an opium bandit through Hickorn's clogged traffic and shuddered. "Twice the motor cylinders, twice the weight? Which accounts for the front-end droop?"

"Yeah, well, it's gonna ride sort of funny."

"That box on the hood, please?"

"You're referring to the hood scoop?"

"I think so."

"Well, we didn't have enough clearance. The engine compartment's kind of cramped. Because of the turbocharger."

"Turbocharger?" Kiet asked.

"A retrofit. An aftermarket kit. The mechanic had one in stock. It was too good to pass up."

"A turbocharger," Kiet repeated numbly.

Binh grinned. "Tromp on the gas pedal and the turbo kicks in. The boost'll throw you back in your seat. We can really haul ass!"

Kiet exhaled through his mouth. "Splendid. Now, what have we learned about our murder victim?"

"Without papers or a face, it's tough. He retains John Doe status. The car was unregistered too. We've narrowed him down to a few local punks who haven't shown their ugly snouts in the past eighteen hours. I should have a positive ID in a day or so."

"Little Big Vinnie," Kiet said. "You have linked him to an American Mafia crime family. It logically follows that senior members of the family are financing intrusion into Golden Triangle opium. Perhaps corroboration on paper of illegal money transfers is a useful approach for us. We may not be able to prove drug smuggling, but we could chop his fun out from under him on a currency violation."

"I'm exploring that angle, but so far zilch. I gather that he's persona non grata in the Cleveland mob."

"He *is* an authentic Mafia gangster, is he not?"

"Without question. I've built a fat dossier. His ex-wife's name is Cookie."

Ah, an intriguing Binh non sequitur. It had been too long. "Cookie?"

"Wise guys marry girls with names like Cookie."

"They would," Kiet agreed, envisioning a Cookie with tattoos, unshaven armpit hair, and dirty language. A Cookie and a pinkie ring; the visible symbols of acceptance in a Western crime concern were indeed peculiar.

"Cookie's the glitch, Superintendent. Her father is the family godfather."

"He sponsors Christian baptisms?"

"No. I mean he's the Cleveland boss. Little Big Vinnie cheated on Cookie constantly."

"With Tess Twitch's spiritual sisters?"

"Yeah. That's his speed. Cookie finally dumped him. Her

father was not pleased. Vinnie's philandering dishonored the family and the godfather."

"He lost face," Kiet said.

Binh nodded. "And Vinnie damn near lost his. Luckily for him, one of his uncles was an influential underboss. He went to the godfather and pleaded for Vinnie's life. The godfather was brutally pissed. He was going to have Vinnie hit."

"Hit," Kiet said. "Whacked out. Zotzed."

"Right on. They compromised."

"How?"

Binh shrugged. "I'm stabbing in the dark. We're talking about essentially a secret society. Their squabbles aren't announced publicly, but rumors sift out. In exchange for his life, I'm guessing, Vinnie agreed to leave Cleveland forever."

"Therefore is it improbable that the Cleveland godfather and his minions subsidized Little Big Vinnie?"

"Not necessarily, Superintendent. Business is business, and these people are animals. They'll do anything for a buck. Vinnie may have given them a shot at turning a hefty profit, and they may have gone for it."

"What did Vinnie do in Cleveland?"

"I'm not sure, but I don't think he was very high in the organization, blood ties or not. He was on the street. A numbers runner or something like that. A glorified flunky."

"Their investment is tripled or quadrupled and Vinnie is reinstated. He is eventually permitted reentry to his beloved Cleveland homeland," Kiet speculated. "Might that be his motivation?"

"Yeah. He corners the Luongan opium market and he's all of a sudden a hero, a rich hero. Could be."

"But would they trust him with said investment? Is there evidence of family supervision?"

"Goons flying in from the States to keep tabs on him?"

"Yes."

41

"Nope. I've been reviewing copies of airline passenger manifests for a couple of months. Zilch. Nobody fits the profile. That's what bugs me, what leads me not to rule out Vinnie being in cahoots with somebody else. He's small potatoes. No way in hell can he be working alone."

"On the subject of bugs," Kiet began, relating his visit to Cuong Van.

Binh whistled through his teeth. "It gets curiouser and curiouser."

"Is eavesdropping paraphernalia easily available in Hickorn?"

"Uh-uh. That type of high-tech toy is spy stuff. The Americans and Russians zap each other's embassy like crazy. Hang around in the electronic cross fire and you'd go sterile, but that's the extent of it."

"Minister Van and I concluded that the gadgets were placed to forewarn opium smugglers."

"I can't argue with you there," Binh said. "I read a magazine article which said that Americans annually spend one hundred *billion* dollars on controlled substances. Tally in Luong's junkies and the rest of the world— It's mind-blowing, Superintendent."

"I read a magazine article which said that Luong's annual per capita income is five hundred U.S. dollars," Kiet said.

"You're a major-league pusher, you can buy bugs. Christ, you can buy the company that manufactures them! Then you pay some sleazeball, say, two grand worth of zin, four years' wages, to plant the bugs. You'll have volunteers lining up a mile long."

"A limitless array of suspects," Kiet said. "A representative of Little Big Vinnie included?"

"Nah. Too subtle. Our John Doe, the headless horseman, that's Vinnie's style."

A uniformed officer entered and gave Captain Binh a folded note. Binh looked at it and said, "Superintendent,

Mr. Taylor requests your presence at the airport, at the air force apron."

"When?"

"At your earliest convenience. It's marked urgent."

Binh's admiration of Tyler Polk (Tip) Taylor seemed paradoxical to Kiet, almost schizoid. Taylor exemplified the righteous, God-fearing, energetic American can-do ethic Binh had grown to revere during his year in the District of Columbia. The man himself was held in lesser esteem. Kiet had not asked for literal translations of references to Taylor as "doofus" and "dildo," but he recognized a Binh cross-cultural insult when he heard one.

"Urgent," Kiet said. "I would worry if I ever received a Taylor summons that was not."

Binh smiled. "Superintendent, may I chauffeur you?"

Kiet suppressed a groan. He could not avoid this treat indefinitely. Let's get it over with, he thought. "Yes. Thank you. You saved me the trouble of asking."

6

Downtown Hickorn's traffic was sweet-tempered and an-archistic. Pedicabs, bicycles, produce carts, military trucks, dilapidated automobiles, taxis, and pedestrians plugged the streets, milling about, darting this way and that on a fancy, stopping altogether in the middle of busy thoroughfares to renew friendships.

Binh, hunched forward at the wheel of the altered Citroën, was frantic. His driving style involved substitut-ing horn button for brake pedal, but the horn wasn't working. His genius mechanic had neglected to attach a wire. Binh's time-urgent agony could not be appeased in the congestion between headquarters and the foot of Richard Nixon Boulevard. Binh's agony was Kiet's salva-tion; one could not exceed Mach 1 in the leisurely chaos.

Bamsan Kiet thought of Quin Canh. He thought of her heart-disease cautions. He nearly chided Binh about the dangers of irrational impatience, of how stress commis-sioned his body to manufacture deadly cholesterol glob-ules. He did not.

When he had rehearsed his wording to minimize Binh's

loss of face, they had reached Richard Nixon Boulevard and Kiet was engrossed in his own mortality, to hell with his driver's young and healthy arteries. The boulevard joined the central city to Hickorn International Airport. It was smooth blacktop, two lanes in each direction, separated by a brushy median, Luong's closest approximation of a Western freeway. It had been an American gift, a conduit for rushing airlifted men and matériel into the capital in event of Communist shenanigans.

HIC was no JFK or LAX, so the highway was lightly traveled, four kilometers of de facto speedway. Binh was at ease now, relaxed in the seat of his four-wheeled rocket ship, no longer perspiring. He looked at Kiet, smiled, and said, "You better buckle up, Superintendent. We're gonna burn some carbon off the valves."

"I am," Kiet said, his belt already cinched so tightly that his toes tingled.

"Hang on," Binh said.

"To what?" Kiet said.

The engine roared. Binh released the clutch. The Citroën's nose lifted, its rear fishtailed. Kiet's neck snapped back. In the seconds taken to gobble a kilometer of the planet, Binh made midcourse corrections and had them tracking the centerline. Insects smacking the windshield died instantaneously.

"The turbo," Binh shouted gleefully. "Did you feel it punch in? Just like being slapped in the ass."

No, Kiet did not feel anything "punch in"; their suicidal acceleration rate seemed constant. He *did* feel the beginnings of seasickness. The Citroën was bucking as if a rowboat floundering on ocean swells.

"Well?"

"Much power. Yes," Kiet said hoarsely.

Hickorn International was soon in view; insane speed had its advantages. Binh slowed. The brakes squealed and vibrated. He bypassed the passenger terminal, a tiered stucco affair lettered H CKO N on the boulevard side, passed through an adjacent gate, and headed toward the Royal Luongan Air Force apron.

Before Souvang Zhu wangled his fighter command, the air force role had been confined to reconnaissance and army troop movement. Kiet saw the majority of the RLAF inventory parked by military hangers: banana-shaped helicopters, plump twin-engined transports, and flimsy recon puddle jumpers that looked in comparison like stunted offspring.

They were hand-me-downs from air forces that could vaporize an enemy city in twenty minutes. The aircraft had in common a sense of exhaustion, of belated retirement. Oxidation dulled their skins. Leaked fluids stained the tarmac. Tires were smooth and underinflated. Zhu's fighters were the oldest of all. But where were they?

"There he is," Binh said.

Meaning Tyler Polk (Tip) Taylor, the U.S. Embassy's senior drug enforcement adviser. Taylor stood outside the hangar housing the RLAF Flight Operations Center, next to a polished black sedan, not quite leaning on a fender. He wore pressed slacks and a white shirt rolled up just so at the elbows. His arms were folded and he was gazing northward. The brilliant tropical sky accentuated his expression, a resolute squint. Taylor was in his thirties, trim and athletic, two to three inches taller than Kiet. He was said to be a skilled tennis and squash player. Kiet envied his posture.

"Immaculate timing, Superintendent Kiet," Taylor said, pumping his hand, then Binh's. "Major Dinh, isn't it? Good to have you on board also."

Binh strained to smile. Kiet knew that elevation in rank had not compensated for the mispronunciation of his name. Unintentional yes, one more Taylor faux pas, but he had nevertheless implied that the sensitive adjutant was forgettable. A nonentity.

"You mentioned in your message an urgency, sir," Kiet said.

Tip Taylor winked and said, "A positive urgency, Kiet. We have a major breakthrough in the offing."

Taylor's winking irked Kiet. It was a mannerism mimicked from Ambassador Smithson, and like his father-in-law, the senior drug enforcement adviser used it often and patronizingly, in this case as a parent promising a child ice cream.

"Regarding opium?"

Taylor winked again, looked at his watch, and resumed searching the north sky. "Better than that, Kiet. Better than that. Bear with me momentarily."

Kiet noticed in Taylor's close-cropped hair a scattering of gray strands. Gray will displace black gradually and gracefully, he knew. Taylor, like Smithson, was a congenital enrollee in an oligarchy entitled Ivy League Eastern Establishment. These people did not get old, they became distinguished.

Kiet did not speak. He betrayed no emotion. He refused to visibly admit that he had been demeaned. Let this man who had been named for three consecutive U.S. presidents enjoy his silly guessing game.

Captain Binh cracked his knuckles and tapped a toe. He was a volatile stew of restlessness, lost face, and immaturity. False serenity and other walls of self-control lay ahead. He said, "Animal, vegetable, or mineral?"

Tip Taylor laughed. "That's droll, Major. I love your wit and, by golly, you've nailed two out of three. Animal and vegetable, the veggie namely our ol' nemesis, *Papaver somniferum.*"

"The opium poppy," Kiet said.

"Prep school Latin," Binh muttered.

"Animal?" Kiet asked.

"The heroin dealer who received his just desserts last night, Superintendent Kiet. I wouldn't have had the poop on the murder if I hadn't read the smoke signals and subsequently put out feelers. I'm rather disappointed that there isn't at least a preliminary report on my desk."

"We are preliminary to preliminary," Kiet said. "We haven't identified the victim. We have no leads yet."

"*Who* isn't central to the issue. *What* is."

"Excuse me?"

Taylor fanned his ears with fingertips. "Hark! The cavalry comes."

Kiet heard the growl of engines and saw on the horizon five black slashes. They enlarged quickly and took shape: fuselages, wings, tails. Air Vice-Marshal Souvang Zhu's fighter command.

Binh smiled, his pained ego anesthetized by the thrill of horsepower. "Throttles to the fire wall at a hundred feet," he said. "Right on the deck. Wow! They're rattling some chinaware."

Kiet covered his ears, muffling the peal of prolonged thunder as the U.S.-built P-51D Mustang fighter planes rushed over them. One hundred feet? he wondered. Lower than that, thank you; he could distinguish rivets on the bottoms of the five relics that had probably helped rid European skies of Nazi Messerschmitts.

They had been purchased from a bankrupt air circus for the RLAF via an American foreign aid grant. The circus had barnstormed Central and South America, giving aerobatic and mock dogfight demonstrations. They had entertained too few paying spectators, burning too much costly aviation gasoline. The fighters were armed by the Soviet Union, an ironic contribution of six machine guns per craft, leftover weapons donated to the USSR half a century earlier in the United States Lend Lease program to their anti-Axis ally.

Deadly and aggressive as the Mustangs were, they did not violate neutralist policy. The Kingdom of Luong respectfully declined military gifts that might antagonize her neighbors. Obsolete as muskets, Zhu's fighters were harmless on an international aerial warfare scale. They crossed no borders. No MiG jets would be scrambled from Laotian and Chinese and Vietnamese airfields, no F-5s

49

from Thailand, no whatevers thrown in the air by volatile Burma.

Zhu engaged the opium trade, an enemy without an air force. So he said. Kiet held that skeptical thought, an earache interfering with his concentration, and watched the Mustangs separate. Four ships reduced power, dissipated airspeed with climbing turns, approached again from the north, wheels and flaps extended, and landed.

The fifth Mustang, garishly painted like the others in the green and blue and red and gold hues of the Luongan flag, hurtled southward at ground level, banked, and vanished over jungle treetops. It returned, boring in on the control tower, lifting an instant before collision—a stunt Kiet had learned was called "buzzing"—rotated 360 degrees, and prepared to land. Air Vice-Marshal Souvang Zhu was not inclined to mundane entrances.

Kiet followed its approach and touchdown, concealing his admiration. Bubble canopy. Bullet nose. Air scoop. Flame spitting from exhaust ports. Clean lines. Simplicity of design. His admiration was aesthetic. Though his contempt for its mission was immeasurable, he believed that this Mustang was the most beautiful form he had ever seen that did not wear a dress.

"A victory roll, Kiet," exclaimed an ecstatic Tip Taylor. "Clue to the aforesaid positive urgency."

"Zhu waylaid opium bandits?"

Taylor winked. "He killed two birds with one stone, if you get my drift."

Kiet thought he had. "The Rouge?"

"The worm's turning on Ril Thoi and his Mickey Mouse war of attrition. He's finding out how it feels to have the hounds nipping at *his* heels."

A worm, a pet rodent, and a rabid dog? A zoo of slang. Kiet sighed and turned away to watch Zhu taxi in. Ril Thoi, leader of the Luong Rouge, was a *lycée* classmate of Kiet and Cuong Van. Thoi had taken to the hills in the mid-1960s to initiate a revolution. It was to be a classical

50

Marxist struggle fought from the bottom up by a ground swell of peasant unrest. Problem was, the starving, oppressed peasantry ate well, were taxed fairly, and were ignored by federal bureaucrats loath to venture from such Hickorn luxuries as indoor plumbing. A college-educated official squatting in a paddy? Unthinkable.

Ril Thoi's war of national liberation was in a stasis of remote ambushes and pamphleteering. His idealism further stagnated the Rouge; he shunned outside subsidies, his dreamy rationale being that when the Rouge marched triumphantly into Hickorn they would march alone and pure, their arms not linked with Soviet or Chinese or Vietnamese underwriters.

A pristine goal, yes, but Kiet wondered again if his former chum had lived too long in the highlands, his brain cells atrophied by a subsistence diet. Ril Thoi indeed dealt in opium, feeding his guerrillas on the proceeds of caravan taxes and modest drug transactions. But he did not deserve this emphasis, this obsession. The Rouge were outsiders, scavengers, hungry recipients of Kuomintang and Shan and Western gangster and Second Military District table scraps.

"I tried to contact Associate Deputy Minister Muoi. He wasn't available," Taylor said. "The man is dedicated and tenacious. He deserves to be savoring the moment."

"A modern tragedy," Kiet said, deadpan.

Taylor looked at him.

Zhu shut off his Mustang. The engine backfired, sounding like Godzilla's cough. The commander of the Royal Luongan Air Force slid back the canopy and dismounted, hitting solid ground in a bravado stance. He broke into an elated grin and raised both thumbs.

"My man," Taylor said, returning the thumbs-up salute. "Bringing home the bacon."

Souvang Zhu was in his forties, an average-height Luongan with a moon face. He peeled off his leather helmet, revealing a receding hairline. Kiet calculated that he had

51

lost twenty kilograms in the past six months. He had been roly-poly, called behind his back "RLAF's only bomb." While he hardly could be called svelte now, his weight was more proportional to his height.

The Mustangs had somehow transmogrified him from deskbound general to a zest-for-life-and-adventure fighter jock. He had exercised and trained devotedly in the air and had become, Kiet grudgingly admitted, a new man and a hot pilot. Besides the twenty kilos, Zhu had discarded his wife, the mother of his seven children. Now he was a habitué of chic nightspots, narrating his exploits to pretty young women, flattened palms swooping at cocktails and ashtrays.

Binh ascribed the change to male menopause, a common malady of the West. Zhu was finding in his middle age youth and vigor, things Quin wished for her Bamsan.

Zhu shook Taylor's hand, then Kiet's. He was wearing sneakers, designer jeans, and a Teenage Mutant Ninja Turtle T-shirt. He dressed like an affluent street urchin, everything about him a hopeful backward shuttle in a time machine. Try as he had, Kiet could not dislike the irrepressible little bastard.

"What a day," Zhu said, addressing Taylor. "The guy who said that today is the first day of the rest of your life, the dude knew what he was talking about."

Dude, Kiet thought, turning for clarification to Binh, who wasn't there. Where? At the Mustang's engine cowling, taking mental measurements, it appeared, while glancing back and forth at the Citroën. Oh, no, Kiet thought. Never.

"That bulge in your back pocket, Souvang," Taylor said. "Is it mayhaps my early birthday present?"

"You got it, daddy-o." Zhu gave Taylor a transparent package identical to the one found last night in the murder victim's car.

"Captain," Kiet called out.

Taylor whistled and said, "Luong White Number One. If

52

there's still any question whether Luong has an up-country heroin lab, this is the answer. Read it and weep. Marshal Zhu, your radio report was coded and sketchy for obvious security reasons. Give us the whole poop, will you?"

"The other day we eyeballed a possibly new trail approximately ten klicks south-southwest of Obon," Zhu said. "We didn't have time then to recon the area. We went in for a better look-see this morning at dawn."

Zhu added his renowned flattened palms to his dialogue. "We bounced a Rouge patrol. Six or eight of them. We took them by total surprise. I'd've loved to have seen their faces! We got them all, strafed them home to their ancestors on our first pass. Stitch a commie with a hundred rounds of fifty-caliber and you tend to fuck up his entire day."

Tip Taylor threw back his head and laughed.

Kiet asked, "The heroin?"

"Hold your horses, Kiet. I'm coming to it. I got on the horn to Second District and they choppered in an army squad to mop up. There must have been more Rouge nearby because they'd dragged off their dead before the troops arrived, but they'd left some of their gear behind, including the dope."

"Inarguable proof," Taylor said, hefting the heroin.

"Of what, please?" Kiet asked, pondering the absence of Luong Rouge corpses.

Taylor looked at Kiet and raised his eyebrows. "Christ almighty, man! The Rouge has muscled out the competition. They're running the opium party. They've set up a laboratory in the highlands and they're cooking smack to their heart's content. Marshal, thanks to you, our task is crystal clear. We finally know how to direct our resources. I'm going to buy you and your flyboys the best lunch in town. Kiet, you and Dinh are invited too."

"No, thank you, sir," Kiet said. "We have already eaten."

Binh looked at Kiet and raised his eyebrows.

53

Taylor shrugged, halfheartedly thanked Kiet for dropping by, and walked with Zhu to RLAF Operations. Kiet and Binh got into the Citroën.

"Superintendent, my stomach is growling."

"So is mine, but not from hunger."

"What's troubling you?"

"Coincidences."

"Zhu confiscating heroin so soon after we did?"

Kiet nodded.

"You aren't saying that there isn't a Luongan heroin lab in the boondocks, are you?"

"Yes and no."

"Huh?"

"In my experience, Captain, coincidences are usually contrivances. I have the queasy feeling that we have been misdirected."

"By whom? Taylor and Zhu?"

"I don't know."

"But we can bet the egg money that there's a lab, can't we?"

"Absolutely. But it isn't located in the highlands. It is here, in Hickorn."

7

The dinner atmosphere was funereal. Bamsan Kiet, Quin Canh, Le Canh, and Bao Canh at Quin's table, plucking steamed vegetables from a communal dish and eating them with individual bowls of boiled rice.

Bao was, as usual, sullen and picky, indifferent to his food. Le, Quin's new boarder, ate with similar gusto, her appetite dulled by grievances and injustices. Quin was a hearty eater who never gained a kilo, but tonight she, too, nibbled without relish, her appetite a casualty of the tension.

This vegetarian fare, so healthful to one's internal organs and coronary arteries, was not Kiet's preference, but he had skipped lunch and was famished. He very much regretted the idiotic pride that had compelled him to decline Tip Taylor's luncheon invitation. He knew that the American had treated the heroic aviators to rich European cuisine, expense no object. For fear of gastrointestinal embarrassment, Taylor did not dine native.

Kiet supposed that they had gone to the *terrasse* of the Hickorn Continental Hotel, where he could have, would have, ordered his favorite dish—Ma San River shrimp fried in peanut oil and sesame seeds, washed down with a bottle or four of iced Golden Tiger beer.

He smothered the bland shoots and sprouts with fiery sliced peppers and doused them with *nic sau*, a fish sauce condiment used as universally in Luong as tomato catsup by Westerners. Spicy and zestful now, yes, but delectable freshwater shellfish the limp vegetables were not. Nutritious, Kiet thought, chewing slowly. Wholesome.

Except for the clicking of chopsticks, the apartment was still. Quin finally said to Kiet, "Hickorn is buzzing over the murder last night, Bamsan. Was the dead man killed because of heroin, like everybody says?"

Kiet lifted his cup and sipped lukewarm tea, alcoholic beverages, including the wonderful Golden Tiger, being as popular in Quin's household as saturated animal fats. He hesitated before responding. Quin was asking him to talk police business, despite their understanding—at her urging, incidentally—that he not bring his work home. Ordinarily he would be angry, but he realized that she was trying to drown out chopstick clicking with conversation. Le and Bao were not sparkling raconteurs.

"Hickorn rumors travel faster than light," Kiet said. "This one is true, yes."

"Opium," Quin said, shaking her head. "It's woven into our culture. To highlands tribespeople it's just a cash crop."

"Old men in dens smoking pipes, dying tranquil deaths," Kiet said. "In the words of my Captain Binh, that is history. Refined heroin is with us and it is a whole new ball game."

"The College of Medicine had another staff meeting on the problem this afternoon," Quin said. "I think that if we can set aside beds and personnel, we'll attempt to treat withdrawal patients. The administrators are willing to on an experimental basis."

Le Canh, Kiet's possible mother-in-law, stirred, rapped

chopsticks on her rice bowl for attention, and said, "Arrest drunk husbands who are crazy to their wives. They ask for a drink in jail, you dump a bucket of water on them and whack their shins with a bamboo rod."

Le was petite, leathery and hard-eyed, a tiny but formidable package. Though unsmiling, she was showing teeth stained reddish black from decades of chewing betel nut, itself a mild narcotic. Kiet said, "Splendid recommendation. I'll look into it."

"Bamsan does the best he can with his many problems, Mother."

"Hah," Le said, sniffing. "Policemen. *Gardiens de la paix.* Bully the drunks like you do the merchants you rob."

"Mother!"

"Excellent idea, Madame Le," Kiet said, also displaying unsmiling teeth. "We public servants always appreciate suggestions from the citizenry. What size stick, please? And might iron not be better than bamboo? Bones break more readily."

"Enough. Let us eat. Our food is getting cold," Quin said, spearing vegetables, setting the example.

Kiet welcomed the silence, the resumption of chopstick clicking. As he ate, he studied Bao, who had not spoken a word, unless his customary sullen grunts could be counted. Leaning into his rice bowl, toying with his food rather than consuming it, he presented instead of a callow face the furry green stripe that intersected his shaven head. He was behaving like a participant in a seance.

Kiet hoped to establish rapport with the lad. To further that goal he had conferred with Binh this afternoon, seeking a primer on the ghastly music that was Bao Canh's undivided passion.

"Plutonium Gecko is kind of a hybrid, Superintendent," Binh had said. "Punk and heavy metal are really two separate things."

"The orchestra's title? Gecko lizards are beneficial. They

crawl on walls and ceilings gobbling insects. But pluto-nium is the main ingredient in nuclear bombs."

"Band, Superintendent. These bands, their names are meant to shock you, to grab your attention. There's no logic."

"Indeed. The differences?"

"Heavy metal is more professional and musical. Punkers talk a lot in their tunes."

"What do they say?"

"Death messages and stuff. Disembowelment and gang rape, stuff like that."

"Ah, plutonium. Radioactivity sounds absolutely benign in comparison."

"Yeah. Heavy metal gets rough too, but they're listen-able."

"Not Elvis or Slim Whitman, either genre."

"You got that right, Superintendent."

"The hair?"

"Those Mohawks. Plutonium Gecko is definitely punk in that regard. Heavy metal groups let it hang long and if they mess with it, it's to bleach and curl it."

"Doris Day."

"Who?"

"Your critical evaluation of Plutonium Gecko, please."

"Earache City. Mom's Café is a bohemian rathole. Gecko doesn't know diddly about good rock and neither do their space-case fans."

Thus armed with knowledge, Kiet said, "Bao. Excuse me. Do you and your fellow bandsmen write your own music?"

Bao slowly raised his head. "What of it?"

"Bao and his friends are very creative," Quin said.

"Of course they are," Kiet said. "Are you presently composing a tune?"

"Yeah."

The boy did not look well to Kiet. His face was unexpressive and pallid. "I know how secretive artists are, but can you tell me the general theme of the song?"

"You wouldn't understand," Bao muttered. "It's too far out for you, man."

"I am receptive to new concepts," Kiet lied.

"Bugs."

"Listening devices?"

"Man. I told you you wouldn't dig."

Dig? Kiet asked, "Insects?"

Bao nodded.

"Insects?" Kiet repeated.

"They, like, propagate. You know, hump. You can't kill them. They cover the world and eat everything and everybody on it."

"A statement against overuse of pesticides," Quin said to Kiet. "I love social commentary in music."

"Likewise," Kiet lied again.

"You people are ruining my supper," Le said.

"You're as dense as he is, Mother."

Quin was startled. "What am I missing, Bao?"

"Grandmother digs. Spray every bug on earth. Poison everybody. We don't care."

"Grandmother digs what?" Quin asked.

"I grossed her out," Bao said, smirking. "You gross out, you groove to the beat."

Kiet sighed. "Whatever happened to blue suede shoes and heartbreak hotels?"

Bao glared at Kiet and impaled his chopsticks in the glutinous rice. In Luong this was a grave insult to the cook, apparent retaliation for inviting such a dunce into her home and her heart. Bao mumbled that he had to be at Mom's Café for his gig. He stomped out, slamming the apartment door.

Le, Quin, and Kiet finished their food in silence. If loss of face was literal, the floor would have been waist-deep with averted eyes and clenched mouths.

Kiet praised the meal and made bona fide excuses.

59

Fatigue. Long day. And thanks to the opium war's treasure chest of bad surprises, tomorrow promised no relief.

While Le cleared the table, Quin walked Kiet into the hallway. The door was left open for the sake of propriety, and Kiet noticed through it that Le's path to and from the kitchen detoured into the living room. He cocked his head and took Quin's hand, taking away also the old bat's angle. Their kiss was a compromise of cordiality and foreplay.

Quin pushed Kiet's midsection with both hands, playfully squeezing his flab, sliding free from the wall to which he had her pinned. "Sorry."

"Likewise," he said.

She smiled. "For how the evening went too, Mr. Dirty Mind."

"Oh."

"We shall adapt, Bamsan. You and I and my family."

"Yes. We shall. But when?"

"After an adjustment period. My son is a gifted brat and my mother is a bitter old woman."

"I recommend a short adjustment period," Kiet said. "Come home with me for two or three days. They will learn how impossible it is to cope without you. They will fall on their knees in remorse and gratitude."

Quin laughed, turned Kiet by his shoulders, slapped his rear, and shoved him toward the stairs. "Go. Begone. I'll scrub the dishes and mop the floor, to work off my frustrations. You bicycle home hard for yours."

Kiet blew her a kiss through a pained grimace, lying by omission that he was bicycleless. He hailed a cyclo dop, a motorized pedicab, and gave the driver his address.

Three blocks from home, they approached a twenty-four-hour grocery, which was another outgrowth of the opium war. The stores served the shopping needs of Hickorn's night crawlers, its drugged and debauched vampires.

Kiet was still hungry, very hungry. Waiting in his freezer compartment was Mrs. Smith's chocolate and whipped cream and shaved chocolate delight. He knew that he would ravage it and that guilt would sour the pastry's remarkable flavor. He entered the grocery and selected from the frozen food case a substitute snack, a barrier to impending guilt.

He haggled with the grocer, arrived at a mutually satisfactory price, paid him, then paid and released the cyclo dop driver. A brisk three-block stroll shall burn many, many calories, he thought, retroactive calories contained inside the carton he balanced on a palm.

Kiet had bought a Sara Lee creation, a cheesecake and strawberry confection. The carton was labeled "light," each serving a negligible 200 calories. That there were ten servings per container was of little importance. "Light" was the key word here. "Light" meant harmony with diet and fitness objectives.

Kiet turned the last corner and lengthened his stride, outrunning his conscience.

8

The morning followed a night of fitful sleep and demonic nightmares. Bamsan Kiet arrived at headquarters an unwell man. A touch of influenza, he diagnosed as he lumbered inside. He belched, tasted strawberries, and chewed his fifth antacid tablet of the emerging day. In Hickorn's tropical heat and humidity, he mused, viruses not only thrive, they revel in a human body as if celebrating on a furlough.

Kiet's desk sergeant gave him a message from the Soviet Embassy. "A courier delivered it fifteen minutes ago," the sergeant said. "He requested—"

"That I call on the ambassador at my earliest convenience," Kiet read. "Before I go, does anything require my attention?"

"No, Superintendent. Nothing important. Graveyard shift had a peaceful night for a change and if an emergency arises, Captain Binh is in his office."

The sergeant spoke softly. Too softly, almost somberly. He was masking amusement. Kiet saw it in his eyes, as he

63

did in the eyes of the clerk behind him, who was feigning concentration on his Underwood portable.

I look as terrible as I feel, Kiet realized. No, probably worse. He was witnessing camaraderie in their bitten cheeks. The youthful desk sergeant and his even younger typist had presumed his deathly appearance to be the consequence of a hangover. Their leader had been out partying until all hours. This camaraderie was, of course, suppressed. A junior officer did not ask Hickorn's superintendent of police whether he had had a good time, whether he had gotten any.

Though Kiet did not care to be reputed by his men as a drunken whoremonger, he did not remedy the false impression. Let the lads believe that their ancient and stodgy superintendent maintained a spark of life, foibles included. Camaraderie.

Kiet winced—phony verification that his illness was indeed a hangover headache—and told the sergeant that he would be at the Soviet Embassy until further notice. He caught a taxi and rode ten streets westward on Avenue Alexandre Loubet in a Renault sedan older than either of the policemen to whom he had shamelessly playacted.

Fiction became fact. The Renault's suspension was as feeble as Binh's souped-up Citroën's and the cabdriver jolted along at speed, oblivious to potholes. When Kiet stepped out at his destination, his headache was genuine.

The embassy of the Union of Soviet Socialist Republics was four stories of imposing gray. Small, smoked windows were inset in concrete. On the roof was a thicket of satellite dishes and antennae. Construction had been less than first rate, and cracks and stains were visible on the walls. Not an inviting place, Kiet observed as he chewed an antacid tablet. Whenever he saw the building he wondered if it had been designed by a gulag architect.

Guards checked his identification, then escorted him inside and up a creaky elevator to a top-floor suite. They turned him over to a stocky middle-aged receptionist who appeared capable of handling any security problem by herself. She told Kiet to sit, rapped crisply on the inner office door, and went in.

Kiet sat. What was her name? Olga, he thought. She was a holdover from Kalashnikov, the last ambassador. Kalashnikov was a vulgar ox, a hard-line Stalinist whom Kiet readily identified with the hammer and sickle.

This new ambassador, this Shiherazade, was the utter opposite. He was slim and urbane and excessively polite. He was a protégé of the reigning president, the *glasnost* fellow with the birthmark and the wife Kiet regarded as beauteous as a round-eye woman could be. Shiherazade had perfect teeth and a glorious smile. He was educated, cultured, and irritatingly pedantic.

The man did not jibe with the stereotypical Marxist-Leninist bent of brutal conquest. He was difficult to pigeonhole, to analyze. He therefore made Kiet extremely wary. He easily imagined the ambassador's pearly incisors buried in Prince Pakse's neck.

Ambassador Shiherazade came out, grinning like a salesman, arm extended. "Superintendent Kiet. I'm grateful that you could take time from your hectic schedule to see me. How are you?"

Kiet read handshakes, interpreted them. Shiherazade's was masculine, yet gentle and brief—a businessman/diplomat sort of greeting. Kalashnikov had liked to squeeze unwary palms into calcium dust and meat.

"Splendid, sir."

"If I may say so, you are a bit peaked."

"Thank you for your concern, Mr. Ambassador. There is an influenza virus going around, but I'll be fine."

"I trust you will and I won't detain you long, but I have somebody I would like you to meet."

They went into Shiherazade's office. Kiet scanned the portraits on the walls. It was the only way to keep track of which Bolshevik was a saint and which was a running-dog revisionist.

Gorbachev's was mounted directly behind the ambassador's desk chair, and it was naturally the largest. Lenin. Marx. Engels. Brezhnev. Chernenko. Andropov. Khrushchev. On the outer fringes, the USSR's Indo-Chinese allies, dead and alive: Ho Chi Minh, Pham Van Dong, Truong Chinh, Kaysone Phomvihan of Laos, and Heng Samrin, Vietnam's Cambodian puppet. Weren't Khrushchev and Brezhnev absent last time he visited? He couldn't remember. But they were on display now, members of the panoply. Had *glasnost* rehabilitated them?

In the room with the hanging revolutionary heroes was a living human being, a spiffy Latino who rose from a sofa.

"Superintendent of Police Kiet," Shiherazade said, "I take pleasure in introducing to you Alberto Festerra, Deputy Agriculture Minister of the Republic of Cuba."

Ah, Kiet thought as he accepted Festerra's hand, Cuong Van's Cuban farming wizard.

"Comrade Kiet," Festerra said in crisp baritone.

"Hello," Kiet said, appraising him. Festerra was thirty to thirty-five years old, curly-haired, trim, of average Western height, and the proud owner of a pencil mustache. He wore a natty gray suit and too much cologne. His grip was weak, his skin baby soft. This tropical agricultural specialist had never swung a machete, had never brought in a sugarcane harvest. He reminded Kiet of a character he had viewed once in an old movie that played at a Hickorn cinema—a tango bandleader. Alberto Festerra had KGB written all over him.

Ambassador Shiherazade said, "Comrade Festerra is flying to Obon today, Superintendent. My government has approved funding for our alternative cropping program. Alberto has been in contact with highlands opium poppy growers and he is in a position to pay money to peasants who consent. America's overture to opium proliferation is predictably warlike. The Soviet people believe that increased food production is the answer. Fill stomachs and provide incomes for farmers, and Luong's drug evils will disappear, thanks to our technical guidance and subsidies."

"Admirable," Kiet said, gulping to suppress a strawberry burp.

Festerra lighted a British cigarette with a gold lighter and said, "Their fields are fertile, Comrade Kiet. With proper fertilization and rotation techniques, they could yield two cash crops a year of coffee, corn, or beans."

"Splendid," Kiet said.

"President Castro has generously loaned Alberto's services to us and to the Kingdom of Luong," Shiherazade said. "The Soviet Union is temperate, subarctic, and arctic. Our cooperatives produce a huge bounty of foodstuffs, but we have no experience in hot-weather growing."

"Yes," Kiet said politely. He subscribed to the overseas edition of *Time* magazine. He knew that Russian collective farms were inefficient disasters. Every few years Moscow bought wheat on the world market. And Soviet aid braced Cuba against a worse disaster—capricious sugar prices in a rudimentary one-crop economy. In his mind he paraphrased a Binhism: visually impaired persons leading around similarly afflicted individuals.

"Since you and Alberto are waging the same battle, the battle against opium, albeit in a different manner, I felt it was vital that you meet."

"Yes." There has to be more to this than a simple introduction, Kiet thought. What was their game? His head throbbed. His stomach was on fire. He wanted out of here.

"I have been informed of two separate heroin seizures in the past two days," Shiherazade said solemnly. "These developments worry me."

"Me too, Mr. Ambassador."

"The incident in Hickorn's tenderloin district, the unsightly street known as the Strip, involved a Luongan mobster and an American urban crime clique."

"Allegedly," Kiet said.

67

"Allegedly." Shiherazade shook his head. "As you wish. Moscow has woes, but thankfully we are not terrorized by gangsterism."

If this preposterous assertion was true, Kiet thought, it would be because there was nothing valuable to steal. "Excuse me, sir. No crime?"

Shiherazade fluttered a manicured hand. "Isolated cases of antisocial behavior, admittedly, but not wide-spread narcotics addiction and rampaging criminal bands. Political criminals, the dissidents beloved by the West, this lawless element tears at the fabric of the state. They are our biggest headache."

Headache indeed. The ambassador was steering the conversation to ideology. Yesterday Taylor, today Shiher-azade. Kiet was being treated to a full range of political zeal and if it didn't soon cease, he would vomit on shoddy, Russian-woven carpeting. "Mr. Festerra, is crime a serious problem in Cuba?"

"Our crime rate is very low, Comrade, and drug addic-tion is virtually unheard of."

I am not your comrade, Kiet said to himself. "Oh, really?"

Festerra smiled broadly. "Not since the Mariel boatlift."

Shiherazade said, "My information on the second sei-zure is vague. Military personnel stole it."

"Stole?"

"Airmen removed it from a cache belonging to Second Military District soldiers who ship and probably refine opium."

Kiet did not reply. Brothers in communism or not, due to Ril Thoi's independent nature the Luong Rouge and the Russians were not friendly. Shiherazade had no real in-centive to lie on Thoi's behalf. And Kiet remained leery of Zhu's story. He was puzzled. Whose heroin was it?

"You did not know or you were misinformed, Superin-tendent Kiet? I am sorry to be the bearer of such tidings. Isn't it ironic, though, that one military faction *allegedly* fighting the opium ring steals heroin owned by another?" Shiherazade's smile was iridescent. Ah, thought Kiet, it's coming.

"Is it not reasonable to presume that army and air force opium racketeers are collaborating with Hickorn mobsters?" Shiherazade continued. "Local hooligans have the connections to sell it abroad."

"Absolutely," Kiet said. "Since Eastern bloc countries have no drug addicts, citizens of these socialist paradises living in Hickorn could not be smugglers or chemists."

Kiet's sarcasm did not even graze Shiherazade, who raised a finger, jabbed it pedantically, and said, "Excellent. You understand. Whom but us can you trust? Everyone else has been corrupted. I marvel that you perform your duties as well as you do, being assaulted on all sides by overwhelming venality."

To whom but us—them—should I reveal confidential information and plans? Kiet thought. Ah.

"Alberto will travel the highlands extensively. He is an agronomist, not a spy, but he is at the wellspring."

"I have eyes and ears," Festerra said.

"An exchange," Kiet suggested. "You make progress, you contact me. I make progress, I contact you."

"An exclusive exchange?" Shiherazade asked.

"Of course, Mr. Ambassador," Kiet lied. "As you persuasively stated, we in this room are alone. An island of integrity."

Kiet stood unsteadily. Flatulent gullibility and influenza, they are my exit visa, the protocol of dismissal be damned to hell. "Gentlemen," he said, smiling affably, nodding to each.

Shiherazade clapped his hands happily and grasped Kiet's. "Superintendent, I am elated and I am upbeat. We cannot fail."

"No," Kiet said. "We cannot."

"Go home and nurse your flu with rest and chicken soup, Kiet. We need you at your best."

"Yes. Thank you."

"Until later, Comrade," Alberto Festerra said behind a haze of Dunhill smoke.

Kiet was on the street before it occurred to him that "until later" was a peculiar farewell. It implied a predetermined rendezvous in the undetermined future.

He hoped not.

9

"We've identified our John Doe," Binh said. "His name is Yung Lim."

Kiet was at his desk. "Good job. But are you positive, considering, that he, uh—"

"That he got himself scalped with a twelve-gauge shotgun? Yeah, ninety-nine percent. It was a process of elimination. He was the only Strip scumbag fitting the general description who hadn't been seen. We hauled in a couple of creeps who knew him. They ID'd Lim from the car and his threads. You remember what a flashy dresser he was."

Kiet nodded, although he hadn't noticed. Distinguishing articles of clothing were part of the whole rather grisly mess.

"Gucci loafers," Binh said. "The sleaze-o had taste."

"And who, please, is the late Yung Lim?"

Binh smirked. "This isn't exactly the surprise of the century, Superintendent. He's one of Little Big Vinnie's soldiers."

"An army deserter?"

"Nah. That's what they call low-echelon Mafioso, the

plug-uglies who do the dirty work. Before Vinnie breezed into town, Lim was a street punk. We have a sheet on him. Three arrests for assault, one for pickpocketing, no convictions. His schtick was yanking Rolexes off wrists. Snatch and dash. The victims were tourists and they were long gone when the trials came up, so the cases were dismissed."

"Mr. Lim's career had advanced," Kiet said.

"Yeah. That red convertible ain't chopped liver. Mazda RX-Seven."

"What sort of dirty work?"

"I don't know the specifics, but I'm guessing he was a runner, an errand boy. Maybe strong-arm too, you know, pushing people around if Vinnie had an ax to grind."

"The kilo of Luong White Number One?"

"The smack is obviously why Yung Lim had moved up in the world," Binh said. "He may have been part of the lab operation or maybe he was dealing. Whichever, he was playing both ends against the middle, cutting himself in for a bigger slice. Vinnie doesn't pay his gofers and muscle enough to afford a boss set of wheels."

A garish automobile, Kiet assumed. "Is any of this provable?"

Binh sighed heavily and slumped in his chair. "Nope. If anybody had stool pigeon inclinations, they don't now."

"The late Mr. Lim as object lesson."

"There you are," Binh said.

"To whom is the automobile registered?"

"That's the first thing I traced, Superintendent. The name and address on the papers are bogus. Lim—I'm guessing he was the buyer—wired cash to a broker in Bangkok. He must have figured he could fool Vinnie by claiming he borrowed it from the fake registered owner he created so Vinnie wouldn't suspect him of skimming or double-dealing. A fatal error. Vinnie's not stupid."

Throughout this conference, Binh had been regarding Kiet oddly. It was the same bemused expression he bore two nights ago at the Yung Lim murder scene when he informed Kiet that his shirt buttons were out of sequence. Kiet had casually glanced at his zipper (zipped), had passed a hand across his nostrils (no foreign matter), had accordingly eliminated grossness as the captivation. What was wrong? He asked.

"Well, the guys, you know, out front, were saying you were, um, sick. You look fine now, Superintendent."

Kiet's eyes smiled. Upon leaving the Soviet Embassy, he had been racked by an abdominal pain unrelated to influenza. It was a hunger pang. He ministered to it at a sidewalk food cart. They abounded in Hickorn, and their cuisine ranged from superb to lethal. Enticed by the vapors of a charcoal brazier, Kiet stopped at a cart on Avenue Alexandre Loubet. This vendor had fed him for years and in Kiet's opinion, the man was every ounce the chef that the snobbish white-hatters in the downtown ristorantes and grills were.

Kiet ate fried rice with *nic sau* and snappy red peppers. He had a side order of dried squid and two bottles of Golden Tiger beer. The lunch was curative. Kiet's flu symptoms miraculously disappeared. Meaningful as it might be to the advancement of medical science, he knew it would be imprudent to relate to Quin the effectiveness of a hot, hearty food and cold, liquid combination in the treatment of contagions.

He patted his stomach. "A short-lived virus. I have recovered, thank you."

"A virus. Okay. Right," Binh said. "Hey, your powwow at Russki-land, how'd it go?"

"Enigmatically," Kiet said, then explained.

"Wow!" Binh said. "Shiherazade and some Cuban he's got on a leash trying to hop in the sack with us. That's bizarre, Superintendent. Do you think they're in on it?"

"Opium? Perhaps. They were extremely patronizing to

73

me, but I gathered that they think we know substantially more than we actually do."

"Yeah," Binh said with a bitter laugh. "Who *isn't* in on it?"

Who, indeed? Kiet thought. Fingertips steepled under his chins, he stared at the opposite wall, devoid of answers. Hanging on the wall was a blackboard. The Frenchman who once occupied this office may have had a good purpose for the thing, but Kiet seldom used it. He deemed it as just another variety of paperwork, which he detested in any form.

He walked to the board and wrote in chalk in a corner: JONES-HICKORN GANGSTERS. Then in the others: 2 MIL. DIST.; SOUVANG ZHU-RLAF; LUONG ROUGE. Then in the open area, randomly: SHIHERAZADE-FESTERRA; SHAN, KMT, OTHER WARRING FACTIONS; MIN. OF DEFENSE (bugging—Lon Muoi?); TIP TAYLOR.

Binh studied it for a moment and said, "Friend, foe, and friend and foe."

"Mostly the last, I fear. Our primary motivation in fighting the opium war, Captain, is to protect Hickorn and its citizens from crime. Agreed?"

"Right on."

"Our alleged allies have primary motivations also, but what?" Kiet connected 2 MIL. DIST., SOUVANG ZHU-RLAF, and LUONG ROUGE and circled each. "One story, two versions. Zhu took the opium from the Rouge. Zhu took the opium from Obon soldiers."

Binh joined him at the blackboard, circled TIP TAYLOR and SHIHERAZADE-FESTERRA, and drew lines from them to Kiet's circled trio. "The sources of the conflicting reports."

"Correct. Isn't it coincidental that Zhu snagged a kilogram of heroin from the highlands a day after our heroin find?"

"It sucks, Superintendent. Someone's maybe trying to misdirect us, convince us that the lab is in the hills instead of Hickorn."

"Splendid," Kiet said. He added a category—POPPY

FARMERS—connected it, SHAN, KMT, OTHER WARRING FACTIONS, and JONES-HICKORN GANGSTERS to those already circled.

"Despite assertions to the contrary, homegrown Luongan opium is insignificant compared to what the bandits bring in from Burma, Laos, and Thailand. The bandits initiate the trade with opium gum. It culminates in Hickorn and leaves Luong as white heroin."

"How about your Ministry of Defense notation? Do you suspect Lon Muoi?"

Kiet shrugged. "He's Cuong Van's ranking drug enforcement deputy. I concede that my dislike for the young man biases me, but he found the bugging gadget. He could have planted it too. So. What else do we know?"

"That we have a blackboard that looks like basketweave straw."

Kiet asked, "We cannot narrow it down yet, can we?"

"Hell," Binh said. "This probably isn't the complete suspect list."

Binh answered a knock on the door and was given an envelope by the desk sergeant. "It just came, sir, brought by an American Embassy employee," he said.

The envelope was addressed to Supt. Kiet, marked "For Your Eyes Only."

Kiet groaned. "Isn't there a spy movie by that name?"

"Yeah. A James Bond."

Kiet tore open the envelope. It contained a single item, the business card of Tyler P. Taylor, Senior Drug Enforcement Adviser. Scribbled on the back of the card was "URGENT—Cathedral 1430 hours—shred after reading."

"What is fourteen-thirty hours, please?"

"Two-thirty in the afternoon on the twenty-four-hour clock. The U.S. armed forces, among others, use that system of telling time."

"I don't understand the shredding instruction," Kiet said. "Am I to rip it into tiny strips?"

"He's referring to a machine that shreds documents. In D.C. you aren't anybody unless you have one."

75

"Spies, you mean?"

"Well, sure, them too."

"Are you implying that other professions have a greater need for document destroyers than spies?"

"Yeah. Lawyers."

10

The cathedral and the United States Embassy faced one another, separated by Avenue Dwight Eisenhower. They were the highest and most ponderous structures in that section of the city. Their styles contrasted, so that Kiet often imagined them in an architectural staring duel. The embassy was an almost-new four-story box of steel framework and reflective glass. French Catholics had erected their ornate stone and brick temple of worship before Kiet's date of birth.

Kiet would look at the one-way windows and picture the building as an army officer, a colonel perhaps, glaring at an adversary, intentions and cruelty concealed by mirrored sunglasses. Odd stained-glass eyes belonging to an archbishop returned the gaze. The building officer's gaze was harmless, although arrogant and preeminent, an effect made possible by twin spires—cardinal's caps—and by crosses at their peaks that were two or three meters taller than the embassy roof's electronic appurtenances.

Kiet's fantasies were unappealing and cynical because he disliked—no, resented—these intrusions on Hickorn's flat and drowsy skyline. And he resented them because he considered them exploitive. Both had been built with cheap Luongan labor. By coolies.

Neither had utilized indigenous materials for major structural components. Stone quarried and brick baked in Europe traveled overland at incredible expense. Glass glazed and steel smelted in America flew midway around the planet to Hickorn International Airport. Half a century between the two monuments: in Kiet's view, no conceptual difference.

Due to Kiet's surly mood, the fantasies were especially graphic. Tip Taylor's summons automatically made him sulky, and the senior drug enforcement adviser's timing had degraded sulk to full-fledged hostility. What the hell was he doing requesting the pleasure of Kiet's company at two-thirty in the afternoon, 1430 hours? This was the hottest time of the day at the height of the dry season, the hottest time of the year.

The tropical sun was vertical, straight up in a cloudless sky. You couldn't cast a shadow if your life depended on it. This was siesta time and while Kiet disapproved of siesta as a custom abused to avoid work, any idiot who ventured outdoors deserved what he received, namely solar rays roasting him as if they were blowtorch flames.

Kiet staggered out of a taxi hot enough to fire pottery and gave the driver a generous tip. He had, after all, awakened the poor fellow from where he squatted beneath a sidewalk awning, his back resting on a cool wall. The man had had the decency not to let on that his passenger was a fool.

Kiet checked his watch. Two-twenty; 1420 hours. Splendid. Ten minutes early by either calculation. He doubted that Taylor would be; it would take only a minute to cross from one sanctuary to the other.

A consolation was the street's snobbish trade. Avenue Dwight Eisenhower was more commonly known as *Le Avenue*, and except for the two monoliths, *Le Avenue* was a gaudy chain of shops and eateries that catered to those who could afford the finest. It originated on the waterfront and the chic sidewalk cafés on Ma San Boulevard, and leisured eastward to International District villas, the lode of its best customers. The cute and exorbitant boutiques unanimously featured air-conditioning, and refrigerated air was Kiet's solace.

He took the closest refuge, which was Double Happiness, an arcade next to the cathedral. Arcades along *Le Avenue* were nothing new, but this one had been redecorated and its roof raised to accommodate upper-level shops and a rectangular balcony that overlooked the plaza and a recently installed fountain.

Double Happiness's remodeling financing was an indirect component of opium war money, Kiet knew. Right now he didn't care. He was walking on marble as hard and cold as ice blocks, glorious relief to his sandaled feet. The air temperature was warmer. A perfect eighty degrees Fahrenheit. Invigorating. Not frigid like the temperature Hickornian nouveaux riches kept their air-conditioning appliances at to impress guests. The way the machinery dealt with the humidity was also remarkable. Kiet felt as crisp and fresh as a florist's corsage.

The shops had changed too. Go upscale or perish—that was Captain Binh's analysis of the arcade redo. That's the bottom line. All the drug money rolling in, they're in a keeping-up-with-the-Joneses mode and if you don't outclass the competition, you're history, dead meat.

Binh loved Double Happiness. He said it was a miniature of a smart North American shopping mall, which was an indoor sprawl of merchants, hectare upon hectare of them. Endless as deserts, prairies, and amber waves of grain, if you could believe the young adjutant, whom Kiet knew to exaggerate occasionally.

Kiet browsed from the plaza. He did not enter a shop or a restaurant. He was an honest police officer who lived on his salary, and the wares that appealed to sight and smell

79

were beyond his budget. There were twenty-three businesses in Double Happiness. They appeared to serve customers who had unlimited money and limited time.

Neon logos announced Rolex, Piaget, Hong Kong and Shanghai Bank, Chanel, De Beers. Stores wooing tourists were short on trinkets, thank you; tiger skins, elephant tusks, and gemstones prevailed. For the time-urgent, takeout counters dispensed crêpes and sautéed seafood in plastic bowls. After wolfing down their shrimp, customers could make a computerized bank transaction or have eyeglass lenses ground while they waited or leave film at an establishment that gave forth a faintly acrid chemical odor and a boast of one-hour photographic processing. Such prosperity, such time urgency, Kiet thought. Lord Opium reigns.

Luncheon hour was past, siesta time present. Double Happiness trade was slow. The photo lab enjoyed some traffic, but food counters were shuttered and clerks yawned behind showcases displaying fortunes in gold chain, rubies, and sapphires. Kiet looked at his watch: 1429 hours.

He went into the cathedral. The atmosphere was surprisingly balmy, perhaps due to the stonework's insulating qualities. It then occurred to him that he had not previously been inside this or any other Christian house of worship. Kiet was an agnostic, and never during his police career had a church been a crime venue.

A smattering of faithful sat at pews or knelt before them. He easily located Taylor. He had conspicuously isolated himself and was the lone Caucasian in the cathedral and, furthermore, the lone worshiper whose head was turned instead of bowed. Subtle, Kiet thought.

Taylor spotted him and moved from a sitting to a kneeling position. Kiet suppressed a groan at the sight of this spy movie cliché and walked forward. How many espionage thrillers had he seen at Hickorn cinemas in

which leading characters chose churches for their rendezvous? How many? A dozen, a hundred?

And was the senior drug enforcement adviser a bona fide
secret agent or a mere escapist? If the former, did the CIA
train their operatives with Bond films and Le Carré
novels?

Taylor's knees were at least on padding, an uphol-
stered board that pivoted down from the pew ahead. Kiet
lowered himself beside him, began to speak, but was
shushed. Oh, Kiet thought, sorry; we are total strangers,
two prominently large men, side by side in a nearly empty
church, ignoring one another, pretending to pray or whatever it is we are supposed to do.

Kiet could not remove his eyes from an icon near the
pulpit. It was the Anglo-French messiah, hideously impaled on crossed wooden beams. He was familiar with the
Christians' Savior, but in miniature, as necklace crucifixes
and household wall mountings. This representation was
man-sized and lifelike or, rather, agonizingly deathlike.
Kiet stared and waited.

Tip Taylor eventually whispered, "Are you Catholic,
Superintendent Kiet?"

"No," Kiet whispered back.

"Buddhist?"

"No."

"Luongans are overwhelmingly Catholic or Buddhist,
aren't they?"

"Those who formally worship are, yes, sir."

Kiet sensed without seeing the shake of Taylor's head. To
look directly at him would spoil the man's clandestine
adventure.

"We're Episcopalian. My family has been for genera-
tions. The Sunday services at Kennebunkport are a cher-
ished tradition. I cannot comprehend how a person can
function sanely in these troubled times without a solid
religious foundation."

Kiet took the statement as an insinuation. "We lunatics manage."

"Oh, go right ahead and poke fun at me, Superintendent. I know you are morally upright and that you have firm secular belief patterns, but God is irreplaceable. Without Him any life contains a void."

Kiet remained transfixed on the son of Taylor's God. *Contains a void?* He wondered how something could hold something that was defined as nothing. Was his English–Luongan translation again faulty? So many phrases seemed to be oxymorons. And what manner of deity would stand idly by while his only child was so viciously tortured? There was a sadomasochistic character to the religion that repelled Kiet. If Taylor had ordered him to the cathedral to proselytize him, no, thank you. He had better things to do. "Your card was marked urgent, sir."

"May I ask, if you have no theological leaning, have you an ideology?"

Kiet suppressed a groan. "Yes, sir. I pray that ideologists leave their zeal outside Hickorn's city limits."

"Superintendent, do you realize how nonsensical you sound?"

"It could be that you do not entirely understand Hickorn, Mr. Taylor. My biggest miseries, the crimes that rob me of sleep at night, are the result of politics and business. And combinations thereof. In the absence of politics and/or business, if, say, a Luongan murders a fellow Luongan, crime resolution is simple. Killer and victim are usually related by family or friendship. The killer either slinks off to his favorite bar, the location of which is given us by twenty people, or he remains at the scene crying and wailing 'Why did I do it?' Easy, simple. With politics and business, my job is infinitely harder. We're talking about money and power. Crimes are complex and elaborate. They have no beginnings and ends. A murder or a robbery is a vignette in an overall scheme. This opium war, Mr.

Taylor, it is the worst. Everybody plays, including the ideologists."

"An extraordinarily cynical philosophy, Superintendent Kiet. Luong would have far fewer troubles if she felt better about herself. That begins with nationalism, the very thing you eschew."

Far fewer? Oxymoron city, Binh would say. The prolonged kneeling had rendered Kiet's calves numb. He could not feel his feet at all. How long was this to continue?

He said, "Mr. Taylor, in Luong ideology and nationalism are opposites, antonyms. We are nationalistic. We love Luong. We love our neutrality. The goal of ideologists, of politicians, is domination over rival viewpoints. If an extreme government ever took over, our neutralism would vanish. Luong would not exist as we now know it."

"I see it every day in Hickorn," Taylor went on, unhearing. "There is no civic pride."

Kiet sighed. He had wasted what he believed to be wise and passionate words. "Captain Binh has mentioned American civic pride. Is this the same as boosterism?"

"You hit the nail on the head. Everybody pulling together, making their community a superior place to live and work and worship."

"Chamber of Commerce," Kiet remembered out loud. "Rotary Club. Fourth of July fireworks. Lions. Pancake breakfasts."

"Boy, I'd go to my grave happy if I could contribute to Hickorn's development of that kind of tradition."

This was becoming maddening. "You said urgent, sir."

"You know, Superintendent, the way the situation is deteriorating, it's shaping up that Luong's only long-term hope is a Third Force."

Kiet felt goose bumps on his arms. "Sir, are you referring to the theory of an alternative anti-Communist government, one that usurps power because the present anti-Communist regime is too weak to resist the Communists?"

"Succinctly and adroitly stated."

"The military is your Third Force?"

"Generally, it is the only faction with the oomph to grab destiny by the horns."

Was this the point, the urgency? Was Taylor testing him as a candidate for a silly conspiracy he was hatching? "Third Force means to me coup d'état, Mr. Taylor. Army colonels storm the palace, shoot the incumbents, and promise free elections sometime in the future."

Kiet was angry. His whisper had risen to a shout. Taylor shushed him again. "I'm sorry. I obviously offended you. You misinterpreted. I don't advocate violent revolution. I have an inclination to wander conversationally and—"

"Sir. Please. The urgency?"

"Dad-Dad's—oops, my father-in-law's—er, the ambassador's computer has been subverted by a virus."

Dad-Dad? Kiet could not imagine addressing Ambassador Smithson with *any* diminutive. My outburst must have jarred his Ivy League Eastern Establishment composure, he thought. A useful fragment of knowledge. "Excuse me?"

"A virus. An alien entry that is inputed into a file already stored in the computer's memory. A message repeats itself until it displaces the original data."

First Cuong Van's office bugs. Now a virus infecting a United States Embassy computer. An electronic pestilence had descended upon Hickorn. "Did the virus ruin every file?"

"No. It attacked mine and mine alone. My drug enforcement program program."

Program program? Was the man's agitation bringing forth a latent stuttering disorder. "Excuse me?"

"My drug enforcement program computer program."

"Ah."

"ECOSIT."

Kiet looked at him.

"E-C-O-S-I-T. ECOSIT is an acronym. Elimination of

COntrolled Substance Infiltration and Trafficking. I created the file and file name."

"Clever," Kiet said, wondering whether Taylor knew that *ecosit* was a Luongan word meaning violation of a sanitary code in which a restaurant employee returned to the kitchen without washing his hands after defecating. Probably not. Rare was the Western embassy staffer who spoke Luongan.

"How may I be of assistance, Mr. Taylor?"

"Apprehend the party who installed the virus."

"Of course."

Tip Taylor winked. "Let me proffer a smidgen of advice. Interrogate your Luong Rouge suspects particularly vigorously, if you read between the ol' lines."

A presumption that the Hickorn Police Department tortured their prisoners. An interesting presumption, interesting and insulting. Kiet had no Rouge guests in his jail anyhow, none that he knew of. "Excellent suggestion, sir."

"To that end, I'd further suggest rounding up anyone with a sophisticated degree of computer knowledge. Delve into their backgrounds and anybody who comes up pink or red, he's our boy. Marshal Zhu and the brouhaha he orchestrated in the highlands, how can we forget?"

"I cannot," Kiet said. "Never. No disrespect intended, sir, but is it really possible for a Communist to break into the embassy and sabotage your computer? Your security is formidable."

Taylor smiled. "They did it on the telephone, with a modem. They cracked our password and the rest was child's play. Hickorn's telephones are laughable, but if our boy can master viruses, he can surely get a dial tone."

Hickorn's telephones were a mess, a French system that had been little improved in thirty-plus years. Kiet did not enjoy a ridiculing reminder of this common knowledge by a foreign aristocrat.

"I know of a Luongan computer wizard. One and no other."

"Who?"

"Associate Deputy Minister of Defense for Drug Enforcement Investigation Lon Muoi."

"That's absurd! Lon's on the leading adge of eradication and interdiction. Look to the Rouge and their masters. Hickorn is swarming with Russians and Cubans."

As far as Kiet knew, the Cuban swarm was a swarm of one: Alberto Festerra. "I said wizard, sir, not suspect. Will that be all?"

"Yes. I appreciate your cooperation. I think we should depart separately."

"To allay suspicion that we are conferring. Of course. A question, please. What was the virus, the repetitious message?"

"A trite plea for universal peace."

"Communist humor," Kiet said.

11

Twenty minutes after sundown, Kiet and Binh parked the Citroën two blocks north of Rue ESPN, the Strip, on a short street adjacent a lush, triangular park. Ma San Boulevard and the river were at the west end of the street. A bronze statue of Prince Savhana centered a five-way intersection to the east.

Prince Savhana was romantically savage atop a rearing horse, sword raised to (presumably) decapitate an enemy infantryman. He and his soldiers had repelled a Chinese invasion one and a half centuries before the birth of Tyler Polk (Tip) Taylor's Christian messiah. The battle was the Kingdom of Luong's last military triumph.

Kiet located a pad of search warrant forms in the cluttered glove compartment, tore off a sheet, and began completing the blocks in compliance with Luongan law. Senior police officials were granted this discretionary power because they were more familiar with what was and was not a crime warren than judges and magistrates, who were, anyway, too busy dispensing justice to be bothered.

"I'm not second-guessing why we're jumping Vinnie, Superintendent. I'm really getting off on it, but I'm sort of curious about how come you had me pull it together on an hour's notice."

The Citroën's turbocharged, eight-cylinder, Chevrolet 350 engine was running, idling. It sounded to Kiet like a purring Indo-Chinese tiger. Behind the sedan were six uniformed officers who gossiped and smoked cigarettes beside three department motorbikes. Kiet printed capital letters in the largest block on the search warrant form: SCARLET MONGOOSE.

He said, "Secrecy, foremost. And I must admit that I'm acting on a whim. I'm disgusted being an observer. We watch the opium trade eat Hickorn like a cancer. We take crime reports, investigate without resolution, and file the paperwork."

"We aren't accomplishing shit," Binh agreed. "Your cancer simile hits home."

"I have been lied to so frequently in the past year that I am not certain that I could recognize the truth if it swerved onto the sidewalk and flattened me. We are invaded by people for and against opium, and I don't know who is who."

"Whom."

Kiet looked at Binh. "Thank you, Captain."

Binh flushed, lowered his eyes, and picked at his fingernails.

"As I told you at headquarters, Mr. Taylor nearly caused me gangrene in the lower extremities, him and his spy church kneeling, and I do not yet know what was actually on his mind."

"That dildo," Binh said.

"We cannot search foreign embassies. We cannot interview ambassadors. We cannot harass high-ranking Luongan bureaucrats and military officers."

"Which moves Little Big Vinnie to the head of the class."

"Indeed."

"We probably won't find diddly squat. Opium, heroin, the Yung Lim hit, anything. Vinnie knows how to cover his backside."

"True."

"But we can hassle him. Rattle his cage. Give him a bad day."

"Hopefully we will inconvenience Mr. Jones."

"There's an ax in the trunk, Superintendent."

Luongan television had recently added to its excellent fare of American frontier adventures a selection of crime dramas. Like the westerns, they were filmed in black-and-white in the 1950s and 1960s. One series was set in the 1930s. Its protagonist was a steadfast and grim and extraordinarily violent federal agent who enforced a peculiar temperance statute of the era. Episode upon episode, he smashed into speakeasies and bootlegger warehouses, wreaking havoc with machine guns and axes. *The Untouchables* was Binh's favorite show.

"This is a search, Captain," Kiet said, striving for a fatherly tone. "Not a raid."

The same no-neck bouncer grinned his same vacant grin and swept an arm toward the Scarlet Mongoose's doors. "No cover charge for you gentlemen. No sir, bwana-san."

Tess Twitch was still featured on the sandwich-board sign, but the policemen had arrived between acts. Engaging the attention of the patrons during intermission was a film.

The color was faded, the sound garbled, the camerawork jerky. On the screen were two voluptuous women, a dwarf, and a mastiff. The only item of apparel visible was the dog's spiked collar. The story line was obvious.

A uniformed officer turned on the lights; a second and third blocked the exits. The movie projector was set up on a card table. Binh ended the cinema interlude by pulling the projector cord out of the wall socket, pulling so hard that the machine overturned and struck the floor with a metallic thud. An all-male clientele occupied almost every table. Not a man budged, not a man spoke. They stared at Kiet, as if students awaiting examination instructions.

Vincent (Little Big Vinnie) Jones did budge, did speak. He sprang from his stageside table and ran toward Kiet, screaming "You outta your fucking mind? Your boyo, he owes me for that projector, and don't think I'm gonna let it slide."

Kiet gave him the search warrant.

Jones read it and said, "This is garbage, Kiet. I piss on this."

"The document now belongs to you, Mr. Jones. Please urinate on it if you so desire, preferably while holding it in your hand."

"Har-de-har-har. Everbody's a fucking comedian. Wanna clue me in what you're after? Like I been saying to you time and time again on account of you don't listen, I'm a respectable businessman. You looking for something, tell me and we go and find it. We do this quick, no muss, no fuss."

"We'll worry about the nature of the search, *Little* Big Vinnie," Binh said.

Jones jabbed a thumb at Binh and said to Kiet, "Your boyo, he got a wild hair up his ass again, that opium thing?"

"Not to mention heroin, scumbag!"

"Yeah, and the guy I never seen before in my life who got whacked out inna street."

"Read my lips," Binh said. "Murder One."

Kiet closed his eyes.

"Kid's got peach fuzz on his chin, Kiet, and the best date he ever had was Mary Fivefingers, and he's doing your talking for you, babbling like a fucking loony. You got things assbackward. Where boyo belongs is on your knee, where you got this string comes outta his back you jerk on to make his jaw go up and down, know what I mean?"

Binh responded with an upraised middle finger and "Sticks and stones, Carp Breath."

Kiet did not entirely comprehend Binh's message, but he was pleased with the restraint demonstrated in its delivery—a thin smile and an unwavering digit. The lad was maturing.

"As Captain Binh stated, the nature of the—"

"Yeah, yeah, yeah, Kiet, you're the good guys, I'm the bad guy. You wanna snoop around, you be my guest. Outside of dust on the windowsills, you ain't gonna find shit. Just make it snappy, okay? My customers, they're edgy, you know. Sooner this is done with, the happier I'll be."

"Since you insist, we shall begin with them."

Jones's lower jaw sagged. "You gotta be shitting me. You're gonna search my *customers*?"

"Too," Kiet said. "Search them too."

"Can you do that?"

Kiet was not sure. The sanction of a search warrant to include persons as well as property on the search premises was the crux of a case now before the Luongan Supreme Court. It had been on the docket for years. Kiet announced his own verdict. "Yes. Unquestionably."

"I know this ain't America," said a frowning Jones, "but ain't that unconstitutional or something?"

Kiet shook his head no.

"No lie? You positive about that?"

"No lie," Kiet lied. "Positive."

Kiet made assignments. The two officers at the doors were to stand fast. The other four were split between Binh and Kiet. Binh and his men searched people, Kiet and his team the premises. The division of duties was equitable; in slightly more than one hour, the groups finished three minutes apart.

"Sixty-six suckers and five employees, four male and

91

one female, the latter being Tess Twitch, who stripped down voluntarily, so I lucked out and didn't run the risk of disease by touching her," Binh reported. "Eleven nationalities carrying twenty-one currencies, forty-four condoms, fifty-six dirty pictures, eight knives, four pistols, and thirty packets of some suspicious substance or other."

"How many of the thirty might be heroin?" Kiet asked.

"White stuff? Eighteen. Small amounts. I confiscated the possible smack and the weapons, and turned the perverts loose. We don't have enough warm bodies at headquarters to book that mob before next Wednesday, Superintendent."

"I concur, but did any of the eighteen happen to mention how the mysterious packets came into their possession?"

"They did, Superintendent, and it was an amazing coincidence. Their stories were identical. Person or persons unknown slipped the junk into their pockets."

"Hey, Kiet, listen up. You been flapping your jaws like I wasn't here, but I gotta tell you, your boy wonder personally searched yours truly. He's got the hots for guys, if you wanna know the truth. You shoulda seen the bulge in his trousers, the boner he had for me."

Kiet glowered at Binh, crude telepathy for *maintain composure or you shall lose face and I too shall lose face*. It was a successful transmission. Binh breathed slowly and deeply, and said tranquilly, "The odor prevented me from getting close enough to Mr. Jones to molest him, Superintendent. It's apparent that he hasn't changed his underwear since he was in reform school. How was your luck?"

"I had none," Kiet said, glancing at Jones.

"Mr. Clean," Jones said, grinning.

"Zilch?" Binh asked. "No suspicious substances, no incriminating records?"

Kiet shrugged. "His office is unkempt, yet no business seems to be conducted in it. There was not even a ledger or a receipt book."

Jones tapped his forehead. "Who needs ledgers? I got one of them photogenic memories."

"How about money?" Binh asked.

"His night manager obligingly opened the safe. It was stuffed with cash of many currencies and denominations, the evening's earnings."

"We know you have books, Vinnie," Binh said to Jones, then to Kiet. "The Mafia always keeps two sets of books, Superintendent. The hidden set is accurate. The one for public consumption is fake. Mob accountants can cook the books like you can't believe."

"Where are your books, please?" Kiet asked Jones.

"You got a hearing problem. I don't have no books. I do my business in my head and there ain't no search warrant in the world can get inside a guy's gray matter."

"Is that your final word, Mr. Jones?"

"Does a bear shit in the woods?"

Animal defecation correlated to accountancy? Kiet looked at Binh. Binh translated "yes" by nodding.

"Very well," Kiet said. "Under provisions of the Hickorn Ordinance Book, I hereby suspend your business license for a period of thirty days, effective immediately."

"Ah, Christ! On what grounds?"

"Currency violations. You accept foreign currencies at the Scarlet Mongoose, do you not?"

"You know I do. Yen, marks, dollars, Thai bahts, francs. Sure. Who don't?"

"Businesses are required by law to keep records of currency transactions—"

"Yeah, yeah, yeah. So hard currency don't turn up on the black market where it does anyhow on account of your Luongan zin ain't worth a rat turd and the street exchange rate is higher than the official rate. I'll give odds one Hickorn business in a hundred keeps currency records."

In reality, one business in a *thousand* complied, Kiet thought. "The law is the law, Mr. Jones. Since you use the

93

mental bookkeeping method, you therefore have no valid currency transfer documentation."

Kiet motioned to the uniformed officers. "Please escort Mr. Jones from the premises and secure the doors. The Scarlet Mongoose is City of Hickorn property for the next thirty days."

"You're gonna pay for this!" Jones shouted as he was led out. "I got friends. You play chickenshit with me, Kiet, you're gonna be pounding a fucking beat."

Outside, Kiet and Binh observed as windows and doors were nailed shut, and suspension notices were posted.

"My compliments. I knew that law existed," Binh said. "Has it ever been enforced?"

"Not to my knowledge."

"Are you sweating Vinnie's threat? Assuming he's up to his ears in opium, he may well have influential friends. Right?"

No reply.

"Right?"

Kiet ignored Binh.

"Wait a second! You're like this when you're testing me. You pull something and do your inscrutable thing, like you're checking if I'm on your wavelength."

Kiet continuing gazing at the Scarlet Mongoose. The officers had taken apart the Tess Twitch sign and were nailing the plywood pieces across the front doors.

"You're forcing Vinnie's hand, aren't you? You're bringing heat on him to learn what kind of heat will come down on you, from who."

Kiet smiled at Binh. He was immensely proud.

"From *whom*," he said.

12

The night is young, Binh said. Your currency records
violation was brilliant justification for boarding up the
Scarlet Mongoose, so could we not go door-to-door, as it
were, and eradicate this blight if not once and for all, for at
least thirty peaceful days in which the Strip reverts to Rue
ESPN? A total cleanup is rather ambitious and off the
opium war subject, Kiet cautioned; we cannot obliterate
sin, cage it inside a building with nails and official notices.
But we have momentum, Binh said: I'm ready, willing,
and able. I do not have momentum, whatever momentum
is, Kiet argued, but I will compromise: another search,
just one. No problem, said Binh, nominating as a target
the Kontiki Klub, the Scarlet Mongoose's neighbor to the
south. The theme of the Kontiki Klub was self-styled
South Seas, he explained. Woven straw mats pasted to
walls, coconut shell ashtrays, bare-titted bimbos in grass
skirts, lots of fruit in the watered-down drinks. Their de
facto motif, the true specialty of the house, however, was
fellatio in upstairs cribs, the blow job as purported art. A
splendid candidate, said Kiet, but do you object to Mom's

95

Café? Well, no, although it's lightweight, a college kid hangout, and while the clientele uses drugs like candy— Binh suspended his objection. Kiet's motive dawned on him. His superintendent was not inclined to reveal his personal life except in summary form and in generalized requests for advice, most recently the query regarding the difference between heavy metal and punk, but what Binh did not know of the woman and her son, he accurately surmised. He warmed to the suggestion of a search for reasons of his own. He had been unable to afford college and had joined the department after secondary school, and he didn't think much of those Luong University brats. Let's go for it, he told Kiet. Let's kick ass and take names.

A roll-up iron gate sufficed as Mom's Café's entrance. The maw was the full width and height of the club, and Plutonium Gecko's decibels gushed forth into the night. Tables of young people were chockablock from the sidewalk to as deep as Kiet could see.

Kiet knew that police presence could induce panic and that a sudden exodus of such mass could also be calamitous. He instructed the patrol officers to wait outside, three on the street, three in the alley. Captain Binh and he would go in and serve the warrant.

"Remove your hat, please," Kiet asked the immaculately uniformed Binh.

"How come?"

"To project casualness. To appear blasé. To lessen the menace your captain's garb represents. We're off duty and are here for a cold drink and the music."

"I can dig it, Superintendent. The last thing we want is a stampede, but everybody knows who and what we are."

"Please humor me."

Binh sighed. He took off his hat and patted his mussed hair, and Kiet realized that vanity was the problem. Young ladies in Binh's general age range patronized Mom's Café, potential sexual friendships that, due to an unsightly cowlick, might never occur.

"These punk and hard rock bands, they attract a following that zonks out on them. Have you been following these lyrics?"

Kiet confessed that he had not.

Binh cocked an ear and smirked. "Dung beetles are eating the Angkor Wat, the wine regions of France, and the Los Angeles Lakers."

"Pesticide overuse isn't Plutonium Gecko's intended statement," Kiet said. "Sensory shock is their goal. A musical ode to genocidal insects is their means. You gross out and therefore groove to the beat."

"Huh?"

The music ended. Kiet started inside and said, "As Bao Canh and I do not communicate, I have never asked the origin of the Mom's Café name. Do you know?"

"The kids think it's avant-garde," Binh said in disgust. "They think the fake wholesomeness in the name is funny and clever."

Mom's Café was long and narrow. An eclectic assortment of movie and rock group posters were pasted on the walls. A makeshift bandstand at the far end was empty. Kiet supposed the musicians were on break. There was no panic, but the young people eyed the policemen with wary hostility.

The smoke was conflagration thick and acrid; the Scarlet Mongoose's atmosphere was jungle fresh in comparison. What did these children smoke? Quin frets about my health, my cardiovascular doomsday, he mused, yet she endorses this loud, choking barroom as her son's bastion of creativity.

He saw a service bar in a corner and an empty table near it. They took seats and ordered Golden Tigers from an indifferent waitress in Western blue jeans and a Grateful Dead T-shirt. Kiet looked around for a person of authority

97

on whom to serve a search warrant. There seemed to be no office or manager. Mom's Café apparently ran itself.

Kiet heard somebody call him and Binh "pigs." Binh calmly said to Kiet, white fingernails gripping his Golden Tiger, "They have this stupid notion they're beatniks, Superintendent. They should be on campus studying. Some of these foxy chicks I see have no business in a dump like this."

"They're regarding us like Martians," Kiet said.

Binh gave him an I-told-you-so look.

"Very well, Captain. Replace your hat."

Binh put it on so fast he raised a breeze. "We probably ought to make our move, Superintendent. I wouldn't put it past some of these punks to sling beer bottles in our direction. They're gutless wonders, so if we get bopped, it'll be in the back of the head."

"I agree. A suggestion, please, on where to begin. This establishment appears to be a single oblong room."

"Behind the stage maybe. They must have a small dressing room for the band and maybe an office too. We should go for it. It's late enough that maybe the band isn't taking a breather. They may be done for the evening and everybody in the rear will be gone soon."

Kiet and Binh went to a curtain at a side of the bandstand. The low roar of fifty separate conversations suddenly changed to a chorus of hissing and whistling. Binh turned and tipped his hat. The hissing and whistling became a crescendo. Kiet snatched Binh by an arm and pulled him through.

But for a vertical stripe of yellow light, they were in total darkness. The light stripe was a gap in a flimsy pair of bifold doors that had been locked from the other side. Kiet shook them, identified himself, and said to open up. A yell, a curse, a muttered and hasty conference, a heavy door creaking on rusty hinges.

"They're bugging out the alley, Superintendent."

"Do what you must, please."

"My pleasure," Binh said as he kicked a hole in a bifold panel, reached through, and unlatched the doors. They rushed into a room furnished with chairs, a dressing table, a wall-length mirror, and a can of Sterno.

"The band," Binh said, looking into the alleyway. "You can't miss that radioactive hair. Whoa! Our guys nabbed them."

"Band minus one," Kiet said, hurrying to Bao Canh.

Bao Canh squatted under the dressing table. A syringe was impaled in a forearm and he was loosening a piece of plastic tubing that constricted a vein just above his elbow. Kiet pulled out the syringe and slung it across the room.

"Too late, man," Bao said, dreamily euphoric.

"How is he?" Binh said.

Kiet sighed and shook his head. "He thinks he's in heaven but he looks unwell."

"You're hot for my mother, man. We're cool. No trouble, no heat."

"This is a regular shooting gallery," Binh said. "They were cooking up when we crashed their party. I guess Bao was the only one who had time to shoot up. They ditched their works outside, but the men are collecting it, the spoons, spikes, and dime bags."

"Dime bags?"

"Individual portions of smack in glassine envelopes."

"The apparatus of a heroin addict, then?" Kiet asked, stroking Bao's forehead.

"I'm sorry, Superintendent. I really am."

Bao was smiling softly, lost in space. Kiet said, "Do you see anything wrong with him? Aside from the obvious, of course. Last night at dinner he had an unhealthy pallor."

"Can't tell. Let's get him out of there, to where we have better light."

They slid Bao out from under the dressing table and lifted him onto it. He did not resist. Kiet was surprised how thin and bony he was; he couldn't weigh fifty kilos.

"What are we doing, man?" Bao asked, nodding. "Up high like this, to fly?"

"I'm no doctor, but I'd wager a month's pay on my diagnosis."

"Which is, please?"

"Hepatitis. His skin and eyes are kind of yellow, see. He's jaundiced. I saw it in D.C. all the time when I rode on narc detail. Hepatitis is common among junkies. They contract it from dirty needles they pass around. You want your fix, you don't much worry about hygiene."

"How could I have overlooked it?" Kiet said. "How could his mother, a nurse, have overlooked it? Perhaps the contaminated syringe is a new cause of the disease in Hickorn, but hepatitis isn't unknown."

"Human nature," Binh said. "You don't see what you don't want to see."

"An eloquent double negative," Kiet said.

"Yeah? Thanks. What are we going to do with Plutonium Gecko?"

"Release them. As you stated, we crashed their party, so only Bao had incriminating evidence on and in him."

"We could make a case."

"No. We make no case."

"Do we release Bao Canh too?"

Kiet considered obligations—legal, professional, and moral—then said, "We have an easy case against him."

"Home or hospital?"

"Home first, please," said a relieved Kiet.

13

They had not searched Mom's Café. They had not arrested drug violators. They had not fired a figurative or a literal shot in the opium war. They had achieved nil. They had achieved much.

Their achievement was on the backseat of the Citroën with Kiet, his head cradled on his potential stepfather's chest. Binh drove. Neither man spoke. Their deed was a substitute for words. Nobody was going to jail, no heroin was intercepted, but an addict had been identified, a sick addict who would be treated and cured. They arrived at Quin's apartment house and Kiet went up to her flat alone.

"Oh, God, what," Quin said in either an exclamation or a question. It was unlike her Bamsan to visit impulsively, and Kiet knew he was doing a miserable job of banishing the grim tidings from his expression.

He walked her down the stairs to the Citroën, walking slowly, his arm around her, assuring her initially and repetitively that Bao was going to be all right, then telling his tale, omitting nothing.

Binh and Kiet removed Bao, who was semiawake and

muttering. "I trust our judgment wasn't too awful, Quin."
Kiet lifted Bao upright, propped him on a shoulder, and
said, "I debated between the apartment and a hospital."

The eyes of Quin, the mother, were red and moist. Quin,
the nurse, took the other shoulder. "You did fine. His drug
overdose isn't life-threatening or he would be comatose. I
want to see this jaundice for myself."

"Captain, thank you," Kiet said. "I am indebted. I'll see
you tomorrow morning at headquarters."

"Thank you so very much, Captain," Quin said.

"Yes, ma'am," Binh said.

They manhandled Bao up the steps to the apartment,
with no help from gravity or the patient. Le and Kiet
exchanged imperceptible nods. Le was uncharacteristi-
cally quiet and passive. She plumped sofa cushions for her
grandson and retreated to the room corner by the floor
lamp.

Quin felt Bao's forehead and studied his eyes. "Binh's
talent for diagnosis is good for a layman, Bamsan. He
spotted Bao's jaundice even though it isn't acute. It's in an
early stage."

"That's the captain's experience with narcotics in the
District of Columbia," Kiet said, wishing he hadn't.

Quin checked the crooks of her son's elbows. "Needle
marks. And not just two or three. I'm a blind woman. My
child could wear an I-am-a-heroin-addict sign around his
neck and I wouldn't have noticed."

She began sobbing and Kiet held her. Le turned her
head, canting it from the lamp into shadows. It would not
do to exhibit tears and emotion to a contemptible *gardien
de la paix*.

Nine Luongans out of a thousand owned a telephone.
Seventeen Hickornians out of a thousand owned a telephone. Quin Canh belonged to each statistical majority.
Kiet said, "I'll go outside and if I can't locate a taxi or a
pedicab, I'll walk to a grocery or a bar and phone for an
ambulance."

"It is a shame you do not have your bicycle with you, Bamsan."

"Um," Kiet said.

Le had gone for a damp washcloth and Quin was patting it on Bao's fevered brow. "We might not have transportation problems. It's obvious that Binh idolizes you. Unless I am mistaken, it isn't necessary to worry about transportation. Look out the front window."

Binh and the Citroën were still there. Binh was in the driver's seat, drumming his fingers on the steering wheel. Sacrificing his rest, he was making himself available in the event he was again needed. Kiet was moved by his friendship and devotion.

Bao spoke deliriously, attempted to rise, but slumped back into the cushions.

"Where do you think he buys the heroin?"

"I hope to ask him that question soon, Quin."

Quin had Bao on his feet. Kiet went to them. "No. I can load him into the car. He's half awake now. I'm a nurse, remember. I handle helpless patients every day. Sit down, Bamsan. You should see yourself. You've wilted. You're exhausted."

"Searching disreputable saloons is hard work," Kiet conceded. "Will you be taking him to the university hospital?"

Mother and son were at the door and Bao was doing a clumsy imitation of ambulatory motion. His mouth was agape, his eyes wide and amused, as if he were drinking in a special entertainment unseen by mortals.

"Yes," Quin said. "I'll be on in less than six hours, so I'll stay with him until my shift. It's high time we get past the talking stage on addiction treatment. Bao's our first case, whether anybody likes it or not. Bamsan, please don't go home. Sleep on the sofa."

She puckered her lips and left. Kiet and Le looked at each other and nodded visibly. Kiet weighed her charms and those of Mrs. Smith, she of the chocolate and whipped cream and chocolate shavings persuasion. She had been exceptionally patient, awaiting his advances demurely and faithfully in his freezer compartment. The body temperatures of the two ladies varied not one degree, he mused, but dear Mrs. Smith was infinitely sweeter. No, he decided, no: I shall remain as Quin wishes. Enough substance abuse for one day, thank you.

He muttered good night to the crone, shuffled to the sofa, and stretched out. In a minute or five or twenty, he was in the twilight between sleep and consciousness. Ideas and minor inspirations often visited him on that feathery rung. Obon, he thought. Obon. Obon.

His last waking perception was Le Canh covering him with a lightweight blanket.

14

"Two impulsive decisions in under twenty-four hours," Binh said. "This impetuousness of yours, if you will forgive me, Superintendent, has been well concealed. I'm not complaining. No way. I dig it. It fits my action-oriented nature."

Kiet acknowledged Binh's giddy babbling with a congenial, affirmative response that sounded like a grunt. It sounded like a grunt because it was a grunt, an unavoidably guttural reply from a taut and constricted larynx that was as taut and constricted as the remainder of his body.

Kiet sat in a state of living rigor mortis in the passenger seat of the department Citroën. They were at speed on Highway One, the Hickorn–Obon highway, ten minutes out of Hickorn, headed northeast toward Luong's second city, 175 kilometers distant. They were still in the Ma San River Valley and the terrain was as flat as a tabletop. Light traffic on the four lanes of macadam was no impediment to Binh and whichever land speed record he was attempting to break. The squarish mud dikes, the boundaries of flooded rice paddies, blurred in the periphery of Kiet's rigid, straight-ahead vision.

"We're blowing out some serious carbon here, Superintendent," Binh said. "A road machine like this begs to be given a brisk workout, you know."

"Yes," Kiet managed.

Highway One was known whimsically as Canapé Road, a compliment to His Royal Highness, Prince Novisad Pakse, who had cagily nibbled at the largess of many nations to finance its construction. The motives of the benefactors swung from the political poles, with official aid program titles such as Anti-Communist Counterinsurgent Mobility to Socialist Partisan Opportunity Enhancement, augmented by the imaginative and usually goofy international development theories of foreign graduate schools of economics.

This was Kiet's first Hickorn–Obon journey by road. They were currently traveling on a segment contributed by the United States of America. Kiet knew that the four lanes and divided median was a bold and handsome style of road design favored by that country's citizens. The gravel shoulders were provided by the prudent British, drainage dug by earth-moving equipment from France. On ahead, toward highland foothills Kiet could barely distinguish because of humid haze, the road narrowed and climbed in switchbacks. China and the Soviet Union had paid for separate stretches, which in toto had been a Luong Rouge shooting gallery until the advent of RLAF Air Vice-Marshal Souvang Zhu's P-51D Mustang fighter planes.

A tire could blow out, the automobile flip, crush its roof and occupants on American hardtop, then burst in flames, and roll off English rock into a French ditch. Whoever had paid for what, the Citroën was traveling much, much too swiftly. "We shall arrive in Obon early, in fact," Kiet said.

"Early? I didn't know we had appointments arranged," Binh asked. "How do you mean early?"

"We don't have appointments, but it would not do to arrive too early."

"Huh?"

"I am asking you to slow down."

"Jeez, Superintendent, the gas pedal's not even halfway to the floor."

"Captain. *Please.*"

Binh sighed and decelerated slightly, lowering the wind noise to typhoon level. He drove in silence for several minutes until his pique ran its course, and said, "We haven't discussed strategy. Going to Obon is a wise move. It's at the root of the opium trade, but what's our game plan?"

"You have an American expression that applies. I forget the exact wording. Hearing and sporting events, isn't it?"

Binh laughed. "Yeah. Playing it by ear."

"Yes."

"Sniff around and see what crawls out of the woodwork."

"Indeed."

"First thing," Binh speculated, "I suppose we'll want to pay a call on the Obon police superintendent."

"No."

"Well, we're in his jurisdiction, you know. Personal contact is common courtesy and he might prove helpful."

"No. Not helpful," Kiet said. "A reliable source tells me that he drives a new Mercedes-Benz."

"Oops."

"Providing you're in agreement, we'll make ourselves seen and ask questions that could be regarded as rude. For instance, who in Obon is especially big in opium these days?"

Binh said, "I would not have worn my uniform if I'd known we were going undercover."

Ah, the young adjutant's District of Columbia training again. In huge, anonymous Western cities, policemen could practice espionage against criminals. Binh brought

107

that notion home with him although he knew better, knew that in Obon the criminal element would easily identify Hickorn's senior lawmen. The Kingdom of Luong was much too cozy for spies and counterspies to operate.

Kiet said, "Not undercover. I believe our ideal approach is to agitate."

"Bend some noses out of joint? Get the scumbag element so torqued they do something stupid and tip themselves off?"

"Splendid. That is a worthwhile objective. Nonviolent confrontation with suspected opium principals."

"Yeah, eyeball to eyeball. Everybody and his brother is pointing fingers at everybody else. We can read these jokers up close and personal and draw conclusions. Are we gonna zero in on anybody in particular?"

"As you are aware, I'm extremely uncomfortable with the debonair Ambassador Shiherazade."

"Right on!" said the stridently anti-Red Binh. "A commie lounge lizard. I didn't know that breed of animal existed until he bopped into Hickorn."

"Alberto Festerra, the Cuban tropical agriculture expert," Kiet said.

"A wolf in sheep's clothing. Didn't you say he was going to Obon?"

"According to Ambassador Shiherazade, yes."

"Okay, Shiherazade's pet Cuban is in Obon and the neighboring boondocks, bribing and cajoling peasants into growing coffee and beans. You don't have to be a rocket scientist to know that's a bunch of bat guano, but how do you peg him?"

"He's no farmer," Kiet said.

"You're clocking him and the Russkis as capitalists? Dope kingpins dealing for fun and profit?"

Kiet shrugged. His seat belt, cinched like a tourniquet, dug into his abdomen. "I wouldn't try to speculate about financial motives, about greed, but politically . . . They insist that Moscow has no addiction problem, that Havana has no addiction problem. A child's fairy tale, probably, but surely the addiction rate is a fraction of New York's or Montreal's or Amsterdam's."

"Yep. Iron Curtain economics are so screwed up, you can't afford a Jones." Binh chuckled. "You'd have to black-market a tractor you ripped off the collective farm to support any kind of big-time habit."

"Eradication of Golden Triangle heroin is therefore undesirable to the Soviet Bloc. Heroin further decays the decadent West."

"Right on."

"Ril Thoi and the Luong Rouge," Kiet offered.

"You know, you're raising a supersensitive point in our relationship, Superintendent. I realize you and Ril Thoi *and* Minister of Defense Van were childhood pals, and I respect the situation, but possibly, conceivably, your friendship—excuse me for talking out of turn—has affected your judgment where Thoi is concerned."

"You are sensitive," Kiet said with hopeful sensitivity in his voice. "I'm sorry you are. I'm sorry I am offending you."

"You're not offending me, Superintendent. I worry. You see him once or twice a year."

"It has been eighteen months, actually. I came home late at night and he was sitting in my kitchen in the dark, petting my cat and drinking my beer. That is the way our reunions are."

"He's an enemy of the kingdom, Superintendent. His lifelong goal is to overthrow His Royal Highness."

"Yes. Ril Thoi can be single-minded and didactic," Kiet admitted.

"You should have arrested him long ago, friendship or not."

"Captain, I could not apprehend him unless I placed my home under constant surveillance. Ril is more patient than the Christian biblical character Job. Ril would wait for the one night in a year or two or three when the men I assign to crouch in the bushes are off guard and complacent. I'd go into my unlighted kitchen and there he would be, my purring cat on his lap, a bottle of my Golden Tiger in his hand, and we would sit together and reminisce."

"Taylor and Zhu believe the Rouge are running the opium show from the highland end."

"I doubt it. Taylor believes anything that justifies his politics. Marshal Zhu is enjoying a second childhood and believes in thrills," Kiet said. "Ril Thoi has partially financed his movement by levying road taxes on opium caravans and perhaps buying and selling small quantities, but he'd rather leave opium alone. It hurts his standing with the lowland peasants who dislike drugs."

Binh smirked. "The rice farmers who are going to throw off their shackles and march into Hickorn with him. His revolution is slower than the Second Coming, Superintendent."

"Second coming of what, please?"

"Jesus."

"Ah, Taylor's Christian messiah."

"Yep. We're talking serious tardy here, damn near two thousand years."

Ril Thoi's thirty-year struggle must seem to him like two thousand, Kiet thought.

"Well," Binh went on, "if you're on the mark figuring that Thoi is a small-timer, how come we're trying to connect with him? And why am I getting the idea that Ril Thoi is your sole objective?"

"A two-part question," Kiet said genially.

"Oh, no, you're not finagling to buddy up to him, tell me you're not."

"Very well. I'm not."

"Yes, you are. We can't cooperate with Communists, Superintendent! We'll be branded pinkos. Fellow travelers."

"I refuse to fret about gossip. Ril Thoi is in the middle of everything that happens in the highlands."

110

"I don't like holding hands with a commie. I hate the thought of it. I feel like a collaborator."

A welcomed opportunity to change the subject soared overhead: Air Vice-Marshal Souvang Zhu and his P-51D Mustang fighters. They were loud and fast and low, guiding precisely on Highway One, as if it were a navigational aid. They would soon be required to adjust their course, Kiet knew, as, thankfully, would Binh. A monotonous and terrifying straight line was evolving into a series of treacherous climbing bends incompatible with an overpowered, unstable automobile. Binh was not suicidal.

Canapé Road was beginning to ascend. Curves were within view and a hardtop maze slashed through rough green hills that impressed Kiet as iron instead of flora. Kiet pointed at the aircraft.

Binh had already seen the planes. He nodded vigorously and said, "Wow! Some guys have it knocked, you know. To get paid for tooling around up there like a bird and maybe some gunnery practice besides."

A rising, left-hand turn loomed a kilometer ahead. Binh slowed the Citroën and downshifted. Kiet exhaled and slackened his seat belt.

Binh said, "Okay, I've resigned myself to you zeroing in on Thoi. So how do we proceed to cut this unholy deal once we're in Obon?"

The prospect of a quick snooze appealed. Thanks to the upcoming topography, Kiet would not die in his sleep, mangled beyond recognition in a high-speed crash. He yawned and said, "We'll play it by ear."

Kiet awoke with a start. He had been dreaming about syringes, miscellaneous weaponry, and men in jungle fatigues who had body odor and no faces. Praise the gods, a truncheon to the face had not jolted him awake. They had thudded over a pothole, then another and another. They were in Obon.

111

Kiet shivered. Obon's elevation was eight hundred meters, its midday temperature a subarctic seventy degrees Fahrenheit. It was the dry season and the main street was equal parts pocked pavement and dust. Lined with tumbledown shops and bars that made Hickorn's Strip seem like a chic Paris boulevard, it dipped and meandered in harmony with the landscape.

Not many pedestrians or bicycles out, Kiet observed. Nor the cyclo dops, the maniacally driven motorized pedicabs. He checked his watch. One P.M. Siesta time.

What an unattractive place, he thought. Opium money flowed through here in a torrent, to be sqaundered in more festive and affluent locales. A foreigner's first impression of Obon was consistent: Third World.

"Well?" Binh asked.

"Please cruise slowly while we look and think."

"We'll overheat, Superintendent. The Citroën's not tuned for thin air, and the dust won't do the engine any favors either."

Kiet chose not to comment on his adjutant's whining. "Drive to the edge of town. It cannot be in excess of two kilometers."

Binh sighed and obeyed, although his clutchwork was not silky smooth. The street was optimistically identified by signposts as Rue Obon Grand. Kiet presumed that Rue Obon Grand's termination coincided with the city limits; dust and neglected paving ended, dust and neglected ruts began. Binh U-turned jerkily and stopped. "Well?"

"I saw three hotels," Kiet said. "The Ritz has the most pretentious name and at three stories is Obon's tallest building."

Binh's eyes widened. "We're staying in Obon *overnight*?"

Kiet lifted a shoulder. "I don't know yet. We must register, however, to demonstrate our seriousness."

"We'll be hanging loose till we cut whatever deal we've come to the armpit of the world to cut?"

"Yes. I think we should establish ourselves in a barroom

112

too, establish it as our base of operations. Recommendations, please?"

"I wasn't reconnoitering bars. I was counting. Thirty-seven of those snake pits, Superintendent. That has to be a world record for the main drag of a two-bit town."

"None caught your attention?"

Binh shuddered. "They're same-same. Creepy Crawly City. The disease you don't get drinking from a glass, you get using the latrine."

"The Shangri-la," Kiet said. "Does that not mean paradise? Utopia?"

Binh nodded and laughed.

"Excellent. The Shangri-la competes with the Ritz Hotel for the Obon pretentiousness championship. The Shangri-la will be our headquarters."

Kiet peeled forty thousand zin from the wad he had drawn out of the petty cash fund in the department safe, gave it to Binh, said to please rent a room at the Ritz, and to meet him at the Shangri-la—

—which neither altered his expectations nor induced him to disregard Binh's caveat about sanitation. It was gloomy, a challenge to the eyes, no spotlights trained on a Tess Twitch. He whiffed the obligatory sweat–urine–tobacco–flat beer stench and (was it his imagination?) an additional tang of blood and smoked opium gum. A scatchy Luongan love song played on the jukebox, the quality of the machine and/or the phonograph record so poor that the female vocalist sounded as if she were relaying the tune through the Hickorn telephone system.

Kiet ordered two Golden Tigers, sans glasses, thank you.

Binh joined him and said, "Sorry it took so long. I had to idle the car for a few minutes before shutting down. You don't, you'll cook the turbocharger bearings."

"Do not apologize. You did not take long. You haven't been gone long enough to register at the Ritz."

"I did register. They take your money and whip a key on you. I didn't have the guts to inspect our room. And I have

113

no intention of doing so till it's dark and I'm semisnockered." Binh raised his Golden Tiger and drank.

Kiet noted the procession of air bubbles rising from the neck of the bottle to the inverted bottom and suppressed a groan. "Snockered is a synonym for inebriated, yes? Pace yourself, Captain. Sip. We're on duty. And please whisper."

"Why whisper?"

"Because whispering is conspiratorial," Kiet whispered.

Binh surveyed the room and narrated, whispering "Two or three geeks per table, spread out, hunched over, you can see their lips moving, can't hear anything but the jukebox, no bimbos making the circuit, squeezing crotches, asking you to buy them a drink, no fun and games at the Shangri-la, okay, Superintendent, you're right on the mark, your typical wise and insightful self, this dump being a hangout for heavy hitters in the business."

Kiet marveled at Binh's sentence, sixty-five to seventy words spoken in a breath with minimal punctuation. He nodded deeply, compressing his chins, a bow acknowledging Binh's compliment. He lifted his Golden Tiger.

Binh clinked his against Kiet's. "Sip. Remain alert. Study our adversaries. Be available for dirty deeds. We cannot fail. They'll be lining up at our table, taking numbers to incriminate themselves."

In four or five or eight hours—who could read a watch dial?—the sun had fallen. It was therefore an aesthetically appropriate moment to examine their Ritz Hotel room. While they were still ambulatory. Golden Tiger was a full-strength beer, Kiet thought blearily as he assisted Binh to the Shangri-la exit, not a watery Western "light" touted in magazine advertising by famished actresses and Yuppie jogsters and facile canines. A foolish error on his part: Golden Tiger could not be safely sipped.

"Shit, Supe," Binh said. "Not one customer. Not one of those creeps got off the dime."

Supe? Kiet was supporting Binh, a shorter, slimmer man whose liver and metabolism were less suited to protracted Golden Tiger sipping than the bulky Kiet's. They stumbled across the street to the Ritz, supernaturally avoiding contact with traffic.

"You were right and I was wrong. This has been a wasted trip," Kiet said. "We were shunned."

"We look too honest," Binh slurred. "We look like honest cops. We don't look like we're on the take or the make. To the Rouge, Ril Thoi or no Ril Thoi, we look like a setup."

They entered the Ritz. Kiet asked if Binh would care to rest in the lobby before climbing stairs. Binh said, Supe, they don't have a fucking lobby, let's go for it. Kiet had expected a brothel crib, but the room was surprisingly spacious and neat—a double bed replete with linen, a dresser drawer, a bucket of water for splash bathing, and several squares of tissue for a toilet at the end of the hallway. Binh was snoring before Kiet had maneuvered all of him onto the bed.

Kiet went downstairs and outside for air. That he was on his feet and lucid was scant consolation. He knew he would be ill in the morning, if not sooner.

The cool night air was as invigorating as it could be to a man who was hungry, freezing, suffering a headache, and drunker than he was sober. Music blared from bar phonographs, a strange medley of competing musical tastes. Kiet heard Luongan. He heard Bao Canh's howling heavy metal-punk. He heard Elvis. Prostitutes of all ages and both sexes marketed their craft in sidewalk shadows and from cyclo dops. Prospective sin and sex customers— 100 percent male and not a bumper crop—roamed and gawked. Kiet, a sudden census expert, gauged the low turnout of johns and perverts as proportional to the population difference between Obon and Hickorn. Qualitatively, however, he graded Rue Obon Grand's nightlife as sleazily inferior to the Strip's. Amateur hour, Binh would say.

115

Two young men, barely postadolescent, bicycled to the curb. One dismounted and walked off. Kiet wasn't paying much attention, and when he noticed the boy's absence, he had vanished, nowhere to be seen.

"Come on with me," the remaining boy said to Kiet.

Kiet looked at him. Skin and bones body, shorts, peculiar T-shirt decorated with seabirds and CANNON BEACH, OREGON. The kid had a choppy you-do-mine-I'll-do-yours haircut and old old eyes. Kiet shook his head and looked away, ears and cheeks burning from alcohol and anger. *What does the lad think I am, a sissy boy drooling after children?*

"Sir."

"Go," Kiet said, avoiding eye contact, shoveling his hands.

"Not without you, Bosha."

Kiet looked at him again. The boy held the other bicycle by the handlebars. He pulled it forward to the extent of his reach. "Follow me, but not too closely."

"Go," Kiet said. The boy went. Kiet gave him a fifty-meter lead, then mounted his bicycle and followed.

15

Streets narrowed. They pedaled through a neighborhood of shops and merchant-class homes, the majority dark and quiet. Streets narrowed further, as did the prospects of the residents; these dwelling styles ranged from One Room Stucco to Packing Crate Expedient. The last street Kiet and his guide traveled became a path. Without fanfare, Obon had stopped being.

The path was not bumpy, but by no means level. They walked their bicycles, the boy leading at a slow pace. Out of respect for my age and physique, Kiet thought. Quin should see me. Bicycling and uphill marching. Fantastic cardiovascular improvement. But would she approve of this particular workout? No. Good intentions, bad judgment. Strengthening the heart muscle that might well receive a guerrilla or bandit bullet anyway. How to render cholesterol accumulation a bit irrelevant: Be stupid, volunteer yourself as a bull's-eye, take a blast through the pump. Kiet did not carry a pistol. His armed and intrepid adjutant was unconscious in bed. A splendid stunt, Bamsan, he told himself.

"Shut up, please," the boy rasped. "Do not speak."

I must be muttering, he realized. Sorry. He trudged onward, marking cadence with the lad, trying to focus his mind on the positive; Quin would approve of that. Did he not address me as *Bosha*? Who else but Cuong Van and Ril Thoi clung to the childhood diminutive? Therefore, this adolescent with the bivouac haircut and the tourist T-shirt, while presumably a murderous Marxist guerrilla, was a temporary ally. And did I not drag a dissenting Binh to Obon to stick my nose in this mess? Self-pity and logic were unfortunately incompatible in a plight of one's own making.

The path steepened and foliage overran it. Invading brush and tall grass transformed the trail into a raggedy dotted line. Kiet hoped that the flora slapping his arms and buttocks was only that. He was laboring, falling behind. Except for a bright half-moon shining orange on the lad's fender reflector, Kiet had no visual reference. To separate, to lose contact with his Luong Rouge scoutmaster in the remote, nighttime highlands, was to freeze to death, to be eaten by a wild boar or an Indo-Chinese tiger, to be captured by opium bandits and subsequently tortured and/or ransomed and/or killed.

Nothing of the kind was going to happen, of course. Ril Thoi would not have assigned a bungler to retrieve his *lycée* chum Bosha. Kiet's aching legs and tummy and the Golden Tiger residues in his bloodstream (he pondered for the umpteenth time why the brewery added formaldehyde and whether it bore pre- and midhangover significance in terms of his mental health) were interfering with cool-headedness. Forget it, he told himself. I am well and my woes are purely psychological, thank you.

The miniature orange was gone. Kiet did not panic, but his legs regained some of their resiliency. He strode forward, head down, that damned bicycle an anchor.

"Oof!" Kiet tripped over the junior guerrilla, who had crouched on the trail beneath a tree overhang.

"Can't you whisper, sir?"

"I've been whispering all afternoon," Kiet whispered.

"Push your bicycle into the bushes and duck."

Kiet did as ordered and asked, "What's the matter?"

"Listen."

He heard a faint *whump-whump* of rotor blades. The *whump-whump* amplified and doubled. Two helicopters roared over at treetop altitude. Ril Thoi must recruit his revolutionaries for their ears as much as their zeal, he thought.

"They come from Thailand," the Rouge said as he stood. "The frontier is just twenty kilometers east of us."

"Thai Air Force?"

"Thai or American DEA. The same. No difference. They dip into the same pot for money."

Machine-gun fire and explosions lighted the sky, shook the earth. Kiet fell to his knees.

"It is all right," the boy said gently, cupping Kiet's elbow. "They attacked a kilometer east and they won't be coming back in our direction tonight."

Kiet stood, embarrassed, thinking that the lad was a hundred years old. "What did they attack?"

The guerrilla fetched his bicycle and shrugged. "Maybe a civet cat ran across the trail and they saw it through their infrared scopes. I don't know."

"Not your people? Not a drug caravan?"

"No. Drugs were moved in that area last night. Informants notified the drug authorities today."

"After the caravan was gone?"

"Yes. We abide informants if their news is delayed or inaccurate. So do the opium warlords."

"They killed your hypothetical civet a hundred times."

The guerrilla looked at Kiet and smiled. "You can't return to base with full magazines and rocket tubes. You aren't fighting your war."

They resumed marching. They continued to climb. The path steepened and vegetation thinned. They entered a

119

clearing and the Rouge said to halt. Kiet and his leaden legs did not protest.

The boy reached inside his shirt and removed a small walkie-talkie. He turned to speak into it. Kiet could not make out the muffled words, though he could see the walkie-talkie's luminescent digital display—a green fire-fly. The instrument was state-of-the-art new and obviously expensive. What was the impoverished and ascetic Ril Thoi doing with a costly gadget that looked all the world like a fabled cellular telephone?

Two guerrillas materialized behind him. They were Kiet's guide's age, perhaps even younger. His guide gave him a black bandanna and said to please tie it on.

"A blindfold?"

"Security, sir."

Kiet complied. They roped his wrists together and began to lead him. He groaned.

"Too tight?"

"No."

"Humiliating? We are sorry. We haven't far to go."

"That would be nice," Kiet said.

"Be cheerful," said the guide. "Chairman Thoi is extremely anxious to see his friend Bosha."

"Splendid," Kiet said, almost meaning it.

16

We haven't far to go tallied to three hundred and thirteen footsteps. Blinded and trussed and led along like livestock, what else did he have to do but count his own footfalls? Half a kilometer possibly, Kiet thought. Hardly a marathon ordeal. But when you are reduced to subhuman defenselessness in the name of security, exhausted and famished and thirsty and already hung over, three hundred and thirteen damned we-haven't-far-to-go footsteps tend to be miserable.

He had on his parched tongue an arch remark about human rights when rope and blindfold were tenderly removed. Somebody held a bottle of Pepsi-Cola, *cold* Pepsi, to his mouth, and said to sip. Kiet gulped. It was wonderful, tangy, frosty. How did they get it so cold? Mountain streams in the area could not have made the ice crystals that were encrusted on the bottle under his fingers.

Kiet belched, excused himself, and asked his hosts when he would be taken to Ril Thoi. Walk in that direction, he was advised; Chairman Thoi desires a private conference with his friend Bosha.

Kiet's eyes were adjusting from pitch black to 90 percent dark. After that wretched blindfold, it was like being bathed in the white-hot midday sun. Light poured on him from a foundry ladle.

He found himself in a copse of tall, spindly trees. Leaves and side branching concentrated high up, providing the twin advantage of air cover and ground maneuverability. He saw canvas tents and lean-tos constructed of limbs and brush. They were cleverly illuminated by unknown means, bright within, neither beams nor reflections escaping. Perhaps battery-powered lanterns, he thought. The area was soundless except for a constant hum. The hum and a slight scent of exhaust fumes made him suspect a muffled gasoline motor. Although the camp was transient, a tactical refuge that could be abandoned in seconds without sentiment, Kiet sensed a vague permanence.

He thanked the guerrillas for the beverage and went tentatively the way they pointed. The camp's site had indeed been cunningly selected, Kiet learned, stubbing his toe on an aboveground tree root. You had just enough room to run between the trees if you knew where you were going. A night raiding party would be booby-trapped by botany, running a natural obstacle course, colliding with closely packed hardwood and stumbling on exposed roots while the insurgents escaped effortlessly. This camp selection was the quintessence of Ril Thoi's revolution, Kiet thought; inconclusive in its fourth decade, yet surviving because of a cunning and meticulous flair.

He came to a tent. He could not knock on a cloth flap, so he announced himself by clearing his throat. A nondescript man in his fifties with a smooth face and wispy black hair parted the flap. It was Ril Thoi, Chairman of the Central Committee of the Luongan Communist Party, leader of the Luong Rouge.

Thoi beamed and took Kiet's hand. "Bosha."

"Ril, you don't change," Kiet said truthfully.

"My rightful cause keeps the lines off my face. Come in."

122

In the tent was a sleeping mat, two director's chairs, a card table, and a portable television set that rested on another device, a black box.

"My headquarters, Bosha. How do you like the austerity?"

The television video was on, audio off, a snowstorm of electrons. It was the camp's mystery light source. "Austerity?" Kiet said. "Your per capita televisions exceed an industrialized nation's."

"Oh, the TVs are as practical as they are decadent." Thoi tapped a Ho Chi Minh sandal against the black box. "A VCR. Have you ever seen a VCR?"

"In advertising," Kiet said. "They'll be showing up in Hickorn stores any day now."

"An excellent training aid," Thoi said. "Our socialist comrades are producing educational videotapes. A North Korean treatment on the fabrication and laying of trip mines was outstanding. Available in VHS or Beta."

From childhood at *lycée* to the present, Kiet was never certain when Ril Thoi was serious. His wit was as dry as the peak of the hot season. His sense of humor, not his sputtering Marxist rebellion, kept him youthful, Kiet felt. The Occidental prejudice that all Asiatics were "inscrutable" indeed applied to Thoi. "The humming noise is a generator?"

"Yes. As you can imagine, sound and fume abatement is a challenge to peasant fighters who have no background in engineering and mechanics."

"Ah, you refrigerated the Pepsi."

They were in the director's chairs. Ril Thoi began to rise, saying "You enjoyed the soda? I will bring—"

Kiet raised his palms. "No. No, thank you."

Thoi smiled widely. "Straight to business, eh? Pleasure is to be postponed. Tap me for what you can, then savor a second drink. You will never change, Bosha."

Kiet laughed. But he was not amused. His laugh was a counterpunch to Thoi's grinning comment. Competitiveness had been forever between them. "*I* am a businesslike drudge? Who studied night and day at Luong University to graduate as a lawyer? Whose political views shifted so leftist that he became his own best client? Who organized a loud and destructive demonstration on the university campus in the 1960s—"

"April 12, 1965."

"Yes. Who landed in the Hickorn jail for four months and upon his release fled into the highlands to form the Luong Rouge? Ril, you have a nerve teasing me. Straight to business, hah! My adjutant has a label for you. Type A workaholic."

"What young Hickorn Police Department cadet on the arresting team jeopardized his career and his freedom by sneaking extra food into the cell to his old pal, a demented Communist agitator?"

Kiet averted his eyes. In total sincerity, he had not been angling for an obligation payback, especially a debt a quarter of a century old. "I—"

It was Ril Thoi's turn to raise palms. "I know, Bosha, I know. What is it about our rivalry? When did it start? In the cradle?"

"Earlier than that. Genes and chromosones."

"We could never play cards," Ril Thoi said, his face flushed with fellowship. "We would throw down our superior cards first. We couldn't wait to win."

Ril was jockeying the conversation from the foreplay of substance to maudlin nostalgia, Kiet realized. Why? He wouldn't try to guess. Ril's dialogue paralleled his field tactics—lullaby the enemy into complacency, attack obliquely, withdraw. For a man too proud to accept the alms of his Communist betters, he borrowed freely from the texts of Mao and Giap.

"The televisions and taping machines and cellular walkie-talkies and particularly the refrigeration, Ril, they seem to me excessively useful as training aids."

Ril Thoi furrowed his brow. "Bosha, are you accusing me of capitalistic luxury worship?"

Kiet shrugged. "As counterrevolutionary as it may sound, yes."

"Alas, true. This generation of recruits, Bosha, they are as dedicated to our struggle as I, but they envision a postvictory People's Republic of Luong that is far different from my model. The Soviets prostitute themselves to the West for grain and computers and hard currency. The Chinese will annex Hong Kong in 1997. Who do you think will adapt to whom? Do not wager on Beijing. Forget Tiananmen Square. My fighters know what is going on in the world. They see example upon example of socialist compromise."

Ril Thoi shuddered. *"Glasnost. Perestroika."*

"People say I am old-fashioned and inflexible, Ril. Perhaps rigidity is a malady of our generation. That boy who contacted me in Obon strikes me as a revolutionary of your era. Brave, serious, hardened."

"He is as fine as they come, yet in a contradictory sense spoiled. After Hickorn collapses on its own decay and is liberated, do you know what he will be doing? He will be wearing tight Levi blue jeans and riding a Honda motorbike. He worships an American rock-and-roll music cooperative named Def Leppard. Yes, Bosha, he fights for the present serf and the oppressed proletariat worker, but what the elite ruling class now possesses will be there when the monarchy crumbles. What the profligate cowards do not loot and take into exile. He wants some for himself. He believes his sacrifice has earned him a later life of soft luxury.

"You have been insinuating that I am guilty of bribing my men. I confess. The earth tilts on its axis and viewpoints shift with the axial tilt like loose cargo in a freighter's hold during a typhoon. You cannot predict behavior, Bosha. You cannot know a minute from now what is important to somebody. Human beings are fickle. You hold your movement together however you can."

"Perquisites, Ril," Kiet said. "You have to remember that any employer gives them to retain his employees."

"I am not a shopkeeper."

Thoi was not quite angry, but his strategy had been derailed. The parley was going Kiet's way. "Ah, you and your crusade are so far above the mundane, you should be a religion."

"You are playing, Bosha, teasing me," Thoi said, wagging a finger. "Don't joke to me about religion. The French priests transformed Luongans into frightened, obedient cattle with their purgatory and damnation hectoring. Religion is the opium of the people."

"Quoted Karl Marx. Opium is the opium of the people quotes Bamsan Kiet."

"Opium." Ril Thoi smiled. "You and your lackey did not drive to Obon on a holiday."

"You know we didn't."

"No more sparring, eh? Cease the dancing. Talk plain. Talk opium. Yes?"

"Please," Kiet said.

"Your fixation on our modern conveniences is tied to an assumption that the Luong Rouge is fattening its treasury on narcotics proceeds. Pepsi-Cola and VCRs. Money is no object. Don't deny it."

Kiet made firm eye contact. "I am a cynic."

"Excellent answer. My answer is yes and no. An opium trafficker is often faced with the choice of a straight track through our territory or a hilly ordeal around us. Two kilometers of safe, easy trail or ten klicks of wilderness. The payments satisfy no capitalistic profit lust, Bosha. Understand that. The bandits see and hear things as they pass through. The payments indemnify us—insufficiently, I should note—against the risk of exposure."

"Then you continue to restrict your opium participation to road taxes and an occasional deal?"

"An infrequent and insignificant deal," Ril Thoi said. "They sometimes have no money. They're moving the drug to money. I don't take credit. I am no moneylender. Using your terminology, yes, I continue to restrict opium participation, but because of the war, there is a craziness, an anarchy. Instead of Kuomintang and Shan warlords coming by at fairly regular intervals, we are confronted by offshoots and strangers. The vilest type of entrepreneur. They encroach on us day and night. We've unwillingly increased our income."

"Ah, your political purity soiled by filthy lucre. Am I remiss for not expressing sympathy?"

Ril Thoi clacked his tongue. "Bosha, you are grumpy. You are tired and you drank too much this afternoon."

"Ril, why do I feel that I did not seek you out, that instead you brought me here?"

"I did bring you here."

"No, I mean from Hickorn."

"As if you were inexorably pulled to my bosom? Opposition and tension between two forces, you and I, is in a certain manner the definition of a dialectic. Combine that with a material basis, opium, and have we not our private form of dialectical materialism?"

Kiet suppressed a groan. His question would be evaded. Ril Thoi was avenging himself for Kiet's banter. Intellectual retaliation. Get him wound up on Marxist theory and dialectical materialism and class struggle and running-dog imperialism, and that would be the finish of substance. "Then may I express sympathy for the men you lost in Zhu's aerial assault."

Thoi laughed and shook his head simultaneously. "A monumental lie! There was no raid. The heroin Zhu quote-unquote confiscated was *his* property. The hoax was a reaction to the heroin you confiscated from the automobile belonging to the murdered hooligan."

Suspicion confirmed. "Ril, does anything go on in Luong outside your knowledge?"

127

"I can't tell if you're facetious or envious," Thoi said cordially.

"If indeed you brought me here on a dialectic magic carpet, it is to—let me guess—reconcile the facts."

Thoi clapped his hands. "Yes, yes. I'm being blamed for too much. I help my cause by helping yours. The criminals of an oppressive, mercantile system are deliberately destroying my reputation and my cause."

"My quote-unquote cause is the eradication of the heroin trade in Hickorn. Frankly, you haven't helped me significantly yet. I never did believe Zhu's story. What else do you have?"

Thoi spread his arms. "You need only ask, but do not expect me to lay a packet of evidence on your lap that you can submit in your neocolonial courtrooms. You are the detective, Bosha."

"Thank you for the reminder. All right, you say Zhu deals. Who else, please?"

"That ridiculous little mandarin, Lon Muoi."

"Associate Deputy Minister of Defense, Drug Enforcement Investigation, Lon Muoi," Kiet said.

"He's seen in Obon a lot. He's into opium up to his capped teeth, Bosha."

"I wouldn't be surprised that the brat deals, but his job necessitates trips to Obon."

"Yes, but when he isn't at Second Military District Headquarters hobnobbing with officers who have become opium millionaires, he and Souvang Zhu are Siamese twins. Concentrate your research on Zhu and Muoi."

"Is Luong White Number One manufactured in the highlands?"

"No," Thoi said. "They reduce raw opium gum to morphine base in the hills, a reduction in bulk of ten to one. It's an uncomplicated procedure these moronic bandits can handle without spoiling a batch. But in the highlands only the Kuomintang and Shan have decent heroin chemists.

Nowadays morphine base goes to the big cities. Sorry, Bosha. Luong White Number One is Hickorn-made.

"Souvang Zhu, that quivering little pile of offal, flew his heroin north, machine-gunned a stand of teak to death, and came home to the lobotomized Mr. Tyler Polk Taylor in triumph."

"Should I be taking notes?"

"Is this the beginning of an outpouring of fascinating crime evidence? No. I'm through lecturing. But—" Ril Thoi raised a finger. "I have a present for you, Bosha, a gift for you to carry home."

"It would not do me an iota of good to ask what the gift is, would it, Ril?"

"No," Thoi said, getting up, slapping his forehead theatrically. "I have been an uncouth host. No. Hospitality takes precedence."

He went out of the tent and returned with a chocolate cake, a knife, two dishes, and two forks.

"It has been thawing," Thoi said. "Sara Lee. An American confectionary cooperative you are known to admire, Bosha. I hope it is satisfactory. We eat, you receive the gift, then we'll lay out a mat for your night's sleep."

Kiet stared out of a child's saucer eyes.

Ril Thoi sliced the cake four ways, a cross. He placed ninety-degree slices on two plates, handed one to Kiet, saying "Please excuse the sloppy carving. Chocolate candy chunks throughout are an impediment to neatness."

Thoi inserted a cartridge into the video recorder. "May I furnish entertainment?"

Kiet was speechless, powerless to object, his mouth stuffed. Someday he would have to explain to his old chum how to advance his sappy crusade. Don't preach to the peasant. Feed him morsels concocted by Lady Sara. Convert crops from rice to cocoa. Prince Pakse's subjects will substitute desserts for staples, will gorge themselves into pimply languor. Thrust fists into the air, affix the

129

Rouge banner to every Hickorn flagpole, and join us for chocolate mousse.

Ril Thoi pushed buttons with technocratic aplomb, looked at Kiet proudly, and said, "I bought the complete series. No series in television history is as gripping and important."

Gunsmoke? Kiet wondered. *I Love Lucy? Hawaii Five-0?*

Thoi pushed PLAY and said, "*Vietnam: The Ten Thousand Day War.* We'll see the two episodes with the happiest endings."

The episodes concerned Dien Bien Phu and the April 1975 fall of Saigon. Kiet watched Ril Thoi watch the footage of glorious Communist victory. He looked to Kiet like some men did when they viewed pornography. There was a pained yearning in his face, a lust that would never be consummated. If Kiet did not regard the prospect of a Luong Rouge "liberation" as so repugnant, he would have felt profoundly sorry for him.

At the conclusion of the second tape, Thoi switched off the television and asked, "More cake?"

Kiet patted his stomach and managed a logy no thank you.

"Bosha, don't fall asleep yet. You haven't seen your gift. Actually, you will receive it when you depart tomorrow, but I want to show it off."

Thoi led Kiet through a hundred meters of trees and bush. Kiet noticed that three or fewer tents and lean-tos were visible from any single spot and that alert sentries were posted in strength. Kiet knew the danger of being caught in a firefight was negligible. The Royal Luongan Army was likewise aware of the hazards and prudently avoided casualties by minding its own business.

They came to a bamboo cage. The prisoner inside was on his haunches, his back to them. Because the cage had the approximate dimensions of a major-appliance shipping crate, the prisoner could not stand. Ril Thoi whispered in Kiet's ear that they should be still and unseen, that the gift's stupefied expression as he was being tendered to Hickorn's superintendent of police was worthy of dawn light, not darkness.

The human gift lighted a cigarette. The butane lighter also lighted for several seconds a handsome Hispanic profile. Kiet knew the cigarette was an English Dunhill. Its smoker was Alberto Festerra, Cuban deputy agriculture minister.

They returned to Ril Thoi's tent. The promised mat was on the ground. Kiet stretched out and said, "Ril, how and why did you capture—"

"He is a bad Communist," Thoi said.

The hard tone of the interruption informed Kiet that the subject was closed. He slept.

17

"Public health inspection of Obon bars and restaurants leaves one whole helluva lot to be desired, Superintendent. They really ought to clamp down on sanitation. On adulterated food and drink violations. Obon's out of the mainstream and they're getting away with murder. Hickorn's lax compared to an American city, sure, but nobody'd go along with this kind of filth. Christ Almighty, I don't have the turista, but name every other symptom of food poisoning in the book and I've got it. I could be a poster boy. I hit the pillow at that fleabag hotel and went out like a light. I'm telling you, we were served mucho more bacteria than we bargained for at dinner."

We did not eat dinner, Golden Tiger gave you amnesia, Kiet refrained from saying. Binh was at the wheel of the Citroën, southbound on Rue Obon Grand. The captain winced whenever a tire thumped over a pavement crack or flopped into a pothole. Because jarring motion caused such agonizing pain, he drove sensibly and slowly, too sensibly and slowly for normal traffic. Cyclo dop drivers behind them, hurrying with or to a fare, shook fists in frustration.

I should keep the lad perpetually hung over, Kiet thought; I could ride with him and not worry so much about an imminent reunion with my ancestors. He was in front with Binh. Alberto Festerra sat in back, unrestrained. Kiet didn't feel handcuffs were needed. The Cuban was bleary, disoriented, tame. Anything but dapper. His gray suit was soiled and he smelled rank, as if his cologne had fermented. He looked like an incompetent gigolo.

"Superintendent, you're awfully quiet," Binh went on after a pause. "You could've knocked me over with a feather when you showed with this—this Communist. If you're reticent to speak in his presence, I understand."

"Not the case at all. Due to your food poisoning, I postponed briefing you. Business could wait until you recovered. What would you like to know?"

"Well, for openers, I don't remember you being in the room last night."

How could you have? "I wasn't. I spent the night elsewhere."

"May I ask where?"

"Ril Thoi's camp."

"Jesus. Is that where you found our esteemed passenger?"

"Indeed."

"I figured you'd turned over a rock."

"Captain."

"I hope Thoi provided a softer bed than the one I slept on at that fleabag Ritz. My back will be sore for a month."

"Softer than a mat on the ground, I trust."

"Oh. Well, I'm assuming that's where you came across Fidel's illegitimate son here."

Alberto Festerra sniffed. "Sophomoric insults are beneath the people in this motor vehicle, Comrade."

134

"Don't *comrade* me, scumbag! You can take your *comrade* and stick it where the sun doesn't shine."

Binh's loud outburst in the confined space reminded Kiet that his present health was also less than ideal. He groaned and said, "Captain. Please."

"I apologize for my rudeness. Okay, Festerra was at Ril Thoi's rat's nest and now he's going to Hickorn in our custody. What's wrong with this picture? I'm missing something."

Kiet rotated shoulders, neck, and head as many degrees as age and discomfort would allow, and looked at Festerra, albeit from an indirect angle. "I too am missing information, Mr. Deputy Agriculture Minister. How did you become Ril Thoi's captive?"

Festerra took a Dunhill box out of his pocket, discovered it was empty, sighed, and threw it on the floorboards. "Soft packages have an advantage. You know when you're running out. Can either of you gentleman spare a cigarette?"

"I do not smoke," Kiet said.

"Smoking causes heart disease, lung cancer, emphysema, and may complicate pregnancies," Binh said cheerfully.

"Sadists," Festerra said, taking an extremely deep breath.

"You did not answer my question," Kiet said.

"I won't answer that question. Nor will I cooperate in any context with your illegal interrogation. I am an accredited consular officer representing the Republic of Cuba. I have diplomatic immunity and I am a political prisoner of a degenerate monarchy. Superintendent Kiet, you're in the worst trouble of your career."

Binh contorted his lips and mimicked flatulence.

"You are no prisoner, Mr. Festerra," Kiet said. "I didn't arrest you, I rescued you. Again, please, how and why did you fall into Ril Thoi's hands, and why is he so disappointed in you?"

135

Festerra shook his head imperiously, his fine tango bandleader's jaw thrust outward.

"Ah, you come to Luong to do us a wonderful service. To induce highland opium farmers to substitute crops. To plant corn, coffee, and beans. Ril Thoi says you are a bad Communist. He throws you in a bamboo cage. Is he worried that your beneficence will undercut his standing with the peasants? Perhaps, but it goes further, does it not?"

Festerra did not answer.

"By definition, a bad Communist is a good capitalist and vice versa, Superintendent," Binh said, rubbing thumb to fingers. "Do you have a little action going, Alberto? Is some of your farmers' fund slipping between the cracks?"

Festerra glared out a window, an arrogant statue.

"Superintendent, I realize you're really getting tired of hearing me run at the mouth like a broken record, but your friendship with Ril Thoi has screwed up your perspective. It really has. We're in kind of the middle of some lover's spat these two half-assed Bolsheviks are having and I can't think of a situation that's possibly any more subversive. Yeah, okay, I've said too much already and like I said, you're really sick of the same tune. If you want me to shut up, fine, just go ahead and say so."

"Thank you," Kiet said.

Binh would not lose face as he customarily did when Kiet rudely terminated a logorrhea spasm. Not this time. Kiet tapped Binh's arm and pointed ahead and to the right. He was not gagging a giddy adjutant, he was bringing his attention to outside stimulus. They were on a gradually curving downgrade, hugging a hillside, a nice respite from the switchbacks. To their starboard, a thousand meters high, on course to Hickorn, were five P-51D Mustang fighter planes, the Royal Luongan Air Force Fighter Command.

"Wow," Binh said. "The sun hitting that aluminum skin and those colors. Sheer beauty. Awesome!"

136

The Mustang's altitude shrank them to a cluster of disciplined insects. Kiet noticed that their configuration was changing from a V to single file. The lead ship separated and banked 180 degrees.

"All right!" Binh said. "He's gonna buzz us. A dollar to a donut that's Marshal Zhu himself. Ride 'em cowboy!"

Binh drove responsibly throughout his torrent of euphoric slang, head bobbing from road to air to road. The shoulder on the right was narrow and precipitous. A corner entered fast and recklessly earned you not just an unseemly skid. It would be a fatal mistake.

Binh smiled, childlike, as the Mustang fattened in the windshield. Kiet was not engrossed in driving: He observed some things Binh hadn't. He watched Zhu's chaperons break off and disappear behind hills. He mentioned that to Binh and saw while he was speaking sparks ignite on the Mustang's wings. He mentioned the sparks too, talking suddenly faster, extending the statement into a question, asking the number and placement and type of North American P-51D Mustang guns.

"Three on each wing, fifty-caliber machine guns mounted just outboard of the prop's radius—holy shit!"

"Zigzag," Kiet shouted, shaking the steering wheel for effect. "Make us a fickle target."

Binh swerved left and right, gravel to gravel. The Mustang approached hot and at eye level, stitching the road with bullets, an eye-blinking eclipse of the sun as it screamed above.

"No hits," Kiet yelled, scanning his companions for blood and Citroën for nonfactory ventilation.

"Dirty son of a bitch dirtbag," Binh yelled louder. "He's trying to kill us!"

"Indeed," Kiet said, searching the sky. "Stop, Captain. Instantly!"

Binh pumped the brakes masterfully, halting the Citroën quickly while controlling its desire to spin and hurtle off the pavement, down the slope.

"Out!" Kiet ordered, setting the example.

Binh said, "Where are—"

"Listen," Kiet broke in. "The other four. They're low. We can't see them, therefore they can't see us, but they'll be here in seconds and we can't depend on these four to miss too. Captain, release the emergency brake and come. The car must be moving. They'll assume we're in it."

"Right."

Hand clamped around a Cuban wrist, Kiet towed a dazed, speechless Alberto Festerra into a clump of brush on the hill side of the highway. Binh released the brake and dove in with them.

The Citroën rolled down the center of the road at a walking pace, accelerating slowly. The four Mustangs came in, one after another, chopping pavement but entirely missing the car.

The long Mustang made a second pass from the opposite direction. Bullets disintegrated a sapling ten meters from the men, but again not a round struck its objective. The four took their second turn. Their marksmanship did not improve either, although a chunk of blacktop dislodged by .50-caliber shells struck the driver's door glass and shattered it.

"Hooray. Dynamite shooting," Binh muttered, squinting through leaves and twigs. "Those assholes couldn't hit their mouths with a toothbrush."

The Citroën had gathered speed, had meandered to the slippery gravel shoulder on the slope side. Zhu's (presumably) ship tried a third time. His aim improved negligibly, his fusillade chewing a spot vacated by the Citroën, which had tumbled into the ravine, struck a boulder, flipped on its side, and rolled over and over.

Binh covered his face with his forearms. "I can't watch this, Superintendent. I *can't*."

Kiet patted his adjutant's back. Fatherly pats, consoling pats.

The Citroën slammed onto a shallow riverbed and

exploded in a geyser of flame and black smoke. Gravity and gasoline had administered the coup de grace, had accomplished what thousands of machine-gun bullets hadn't.

Binh's eyes were damp. He said, "The money and work that went into that machine, Superintendent. I don't believe this. I refuse to believe it's happening. They didn't fire a round into our Citroën. Christ, we could've driven to Hickorn and paid them no never mind. The way they shoot, being in that car was safer than spending the rest of your life in a bomb shelter."

"Live in the Citroën, live a life of driving around while shot at by Zhu and his RLAF Fighter Command," Kiet said, suddenly amused. "Twenty-four hours a day, seven days a week. We'd be immortal."

Binh laughed. Good, Kiet thought. Splendid. Never had humor been such a precious commodity.

The Mustangs circled to gain altitude and duplicated their Hickorn-bound V. The forward ship, the V's tip, rotated 360 degrees on its longitudinal axis.

"A victory roll," Binh said, frowning in disbelief. "Zhu has the balls to do a victory roll. That phony bastard."

Phony, Kiet thought. Unquestionably. A male-menopaused, pseudofighter ace. A dismal marksman and a cheater. In a real war he'd claim a hundred kills per mission. Air Vice-Marshal Souvang Zhu, the probable spearhead of Tip Taylor's "Third Force." The thought was uplifting; the Kingdom of Luong was resilient enough to repel a coup d'état by that breed.

"What now, Superintendent?" Binh asked.

"We wait. Vehicles will pass. Marshal Zhu has cleansed Highway One. He has made civilian travel perfectly safe. We'll commandeer something."

Alberto Festerra touched a pocket, reaching for a cigarette he didn't have. "They tried to have me killed, Kiet. You're responsible for me. You must protect me."

Festerra's eyes seemed larger than his face. Kiet could

hear his breathing. "You, Mr. Minister? Our automobile was the target practice. Who is *they*, please? You imply that Zhu has a client."

"Why would they kill you? The police, the air force, you're on the same side. You have the same vested interest in preserving corrupt despotism and opium profits."

"Why don't you just save your commie slogans for somebody who cares, Comrade Shithead?"

Festerra pointed at Binh and said to Kiet, "You, sir, are derelict for permitting him to slander—"

"Captain Binh made a splendid suggestion, Mr. Minister. Dogma belongs in coffeehouse debates, not in remote hills a few moments following a death escape.

"Now, I confess that I haven't an inkling why Zhu wishes Captain Binh and me dead, but the attack leaves me a little suspicious that he does."

"They bracketed in on the car," Binh said. "They couldn't see the occupants from the air, but they knew the car and who it belonged to. A customized Citroën isn't what you'd call common. The hood scoop was like a trademark."

"Agents saw me board your auto in Obon," Festerra said.

"Perhaps," Kiet conceded with a listless shrug. "What agents?"

Festerra studied manicured fingernails.

"No comment? I don't mind. I have time. We are, at your insistence, your protectors, yes?"

Festerra had produced a fingernail file. He dug out dirt and smoothed edges roughened by their adventure. Clearly, this tropical agriculture specialist lacked affection for soil.

Kiet did not press. He was a patient man and the Cuban was frightened. Kiet would stall, would delay taking him to the Soviet Embassy. They would chat later.

They remained partially hidden for an hour, visually interviewing the traffic. Six vehicles passed. Kiet rejected two buses, a truck that by its caged bed and aroma had doubtless discharged live chickens at Obon's central market, a Mercedes-Benz sedan containing an army colonel and a young lady who could have been his daughter but probably wasn't, a Hickorn taxicab, and a massive rust-pocked, tail-finned convertible driven by an elderly, cigar-chomping man.

Binh told Kiet that the convertible was a 1960 Buick Invicta. The convertible reminded Binh that, you know, Yung Lim's car was also a convertible. A fateful coincidence. A red Mazda RX-7, by the way. Like new, cherry, impounded at headquarters, parked in the lot, a helluva waste sitting there like it was, cars not driven deteriorate like inactive people, you know, the gaskets and seals seeping fluids, a year afterward a hunk of scrap metal is what you've got.

Available, ready, not quite as quick off the line as the Citroën, but really cool nevertheless, a helluva classy replacement, a departmental image enhancer if there ever was one. I mean, are we talking fateful coincidence or what, Superintendent?

Kiet said he'd think about it, and then—a fateful coincidence?—spotted their transportation. He stepped onto Highway One, held up his wallet badge, and waved. A rusty truck of obscure vintage stopped. Its diesel fumes were noxious and the cry of metal-to-metal brake surfaces made Kiet's teeth ache. In the cab was a man, woman, and child. They had smudged faces and blackened clothing. The truck's box was loaded with charcoal, Hickorn's principal household cooking fuel.

Kiet spoke to the driver, a friendly smiling fellow, and learned that they were a family hauling charcoal to a Hickorn wholesaler. And yes, the stranded trio was welcome to ride along.

"What are you waiting for?" Kiet asked Festerra.

"Aren't the woman and child getting in the rear? They already look like tar babies."

"We're guests," Kiet said. "We ride in back. They're sooty because they loaded the truck themselves. They aren't afraid of soiled hands. Besides, we'll have a roof over us. Concealment. Zhu and his friends may refuel and have another look. It's better to be dirty than dead. Hopefully we can deliver you to Ambassador Shiherazade intact."

"No!"

"No?" Kiet said, startled. "An emphatic no. Why, please? Is he also one of your mysterious agents?"

Festerra climbed into the charcoal truck.

18

The charcoal truck broke down twice. Kiet and Binh assisted the driver, while Festerra stayed put, a petulant mute. They were not mechanics, nor was the trucker, but the malfunctions were obvious. A split radiator hose. A cracked distributor cap. Rags torn into strips and knotted tightly served as temporary bandages.

During repairs, Kiet and Binh talked out of earshot of their primary problem. Binh's postadolescent heartache over the loss of the hot rod Citroën had subsided and he did not speak of red convertibles. He was once again a working detective.

"What are we going to do with the Cuban, Superintendent? He's paranoid. He's afraid of everybody. He came unglued when you mentioned the Russkis."

"Our jail would afford him the protection he craves."

"Every commie diplomat in town would be on us like a bad smell."

"Alas, yes. Defection to a Western embassy would be out of the question too. He trusts no one."

143

"We could beeline to Hickorn International and stick him on a plane."

"No. For the same reason we must discourage defection. Even if he demanded one of those options, I would play for time. He can't talk to us if he is inside an embassy or in Havana."

"He's not exactly what you'd call a stool pigeon now, Superintendent."

"Patience."

"Truth serum and bamboo splinters."

"You're joking, of course."

"Unfortunately."

"I have an idea. Nobody would dream that Señor Festerra would be secreted there, and he might find the environment agreeable," Kiet said, telling Binh his idea.

"You're joking, of course."

"No."

Binh thought for a moment. "It's goofy, Superintendent. Totally off-the-wall. And we're violating department regs and diplomatic treaties as long as your arm."

"Yes."

"I love it. Let's go for it."

The truck's breakdowns were opportune. Stoppages and a maximum speed of forty kilometers per hour brought them wheezing and steaming into Hickorn after sundown. Black as the trucker's cargo, they blended with the night, three malodorous minstrels who were not eager to attract attention. One, two, or three of us are wished or presumed dead, Kiet reminded.

They hailed a taxicab, then another that had been cruising behind it. Binh, a satirical manservant, opened a door and gestured extravagantly to the Cuban. Festerra looked longingly at Kiet, as if he were a child being torn from its mother's breast.

"Go," Kiet said. "Everything is fine. I'll be around in a while."

"Go where?"

"He speaks," Binh said, looking upward. "We've witnessed a miracle."

"To safety."

"Where?"

Binh had Festerra by the arm. "You'll dig it, Alberto. It'll be more fun than Disneyland."

Who/what/where is a Disneyland? Kiet said, "Have a nice evening, Mr. Minister."

Kiet got into the second taxi. His address nearly escaped his lips. No. Souvang Zhu's colleagues, whoever they were, could have his home under surveillance. Corpses could not have been seen from the air, could not have been verified in the Citroën fireball and checked off an order blank. A wise assassin was a conscientious assassin. Slipshod killing contracts were subject to complaint by both the client and the undead dead person.

Festerra's paranoia was infectious, Kiet thought. A disease of the spirit. He shivered. He was going crazy. This wretched damned beastly inhuman avaricious endless insoluble opium war would have him in an asylum yet.

He gave Quin's address. The driver slowed at her apartment house. Quin's lights were off. Kiet developed goose bumps. Where was she? Then he remembered. Bao. Luong University Hospital. While the green-haired lad would never be a son to him, he was suffering heroin withdrawal and his agony should not have slipped his memory. A P-51D Mustang strafing was not a valid excuse. Kiet felt as guilty as he had in some time.

"Sorry," he said. "Take me to the university instead."

"Don't be sorry, sir," the driver said, caressing his meter. "Wherever we go, for however long, the numbers turn."

* * *

Luong University was founded in 1909 by the French to train Luongans for the civil service. Until Independence in 1954 it manufactured clerks and little else, middle- and upper-class male youths of dubious ability whose diplomas were admittance to a ministry office. A wellborn native had ahead of him a desk, daily dress of white shirt and black necktie, a three-hour lunch and siesta, a ceiling fan, an antiseptic distance between himself and his countrymen, four decades of employment security, and a pension.

The most punctilious of them could initiate a document and give it eternal life. The most unctuous and toadying won powerless promotions that granted tennis privileges at the French clubs. In the late 1940s, an abundance of aristocratic officials with meaningless titles played very often and very well. It was said then that Luongans had the best backhands in Southeast Asia. There was talk of a Davis Cup team.

The era and the curriculum had changed, but clerks were still schooled in the College of Government Administration. Half the student body was enrolled in Admin, Quin complained; we in the medical school fight brain death, they teach it as an academic major.

Degree courses were offered in business and engineering, though, and the parasitology department of the College of Medicine was among the Far East's finest. Perhaps the fledgling drug addiction department will be forced to achieve similar excellence, Kiet thought sourly as he paid the taxi driver.

The university grounds were lush and green, the red-tiled buildings low and open. French architects had paid heed to the tropical climate.

A night breeze wafting through trees was almost cooling. Kiet fluttered his charcoal-blackened shirt as he walked, hoping to evaporate perspiration. He ran a hand

146

through moist and caked hair. He did not suppose that he smelled any better than he looked.

A cross-shape structure housed the hospital and the medical school. Remodeling and expansion was done when they grew out of space, with no long-range blueprint, so the cross was asymmetrical and the interior a maze. As Quin both taught nursing and practiced it, and might be with Bao in a room separate from her normal working stations, he hadn't an inkling where to locate her.

Kiet entered a side door, figuring to prowl for her on his own. He did not want to call undue attention to himself by making formal inquiries. Low profile, Binh called it. Anonymity aside, he was quite aware that he could pass for a savage and that he broadcasted the aroma of a water buffalo. With luck, he thought, I will be disregarded, mistaken for an ambulatory burn patient.

Luck evaded him. People in the hallways did too. On the faces of white-clad staff and green-gowned patients alike were not the expressions of revulsion he had anticipated, but rather frozen stares of horror. Kiet was mortified. He avoided mirrors. Have I ever done anything sillier than rush here without tidying up? he asked himself.

He trapped a rotund physician too portly and slow to sidle by him and asked Quin's whereabouts. Speaking as fast as humanly possible, the doctor instructed him to the next right turn, the fourth door from the end.

There was no name or number on the door. Kiet walked into a tiny anteroom. The walls were unadorned and two folding chairs constituted the furnishings. In one of the chairs sat Le Canh. She looked at Kiet, gasped, and put a hand over her mouth so hard she gave herself a slap.

Not the warmest greeting, Kiet mused. But the image of the crone muzzling herself appealed. Le regained her composure and shouted to her daughter.

Quin came out of the inner room, saw Kiet, and lunged, throwing her arms around him. "Oh, God, Bamsan! They said you were dead!"

147

She began crying so intensely that she felt to Kiet as if she were convulsing. He stroked her back while edging the two of them to the remaining chair. He eased into it, bringing Quin onto his lap. She spoke, but the mix of language and sobbing was unintelligible.

"It was on the radio," Le interpreted. "Opium bandits ambushed your car on Highway One outside of Obon. They shot you and your adjutant and a Cuban to death. They poured gasoline on the car, you in it, and shoved it over a cliff. That fat little air force general who plays in old airplanes, what's his name?"

"Air Vice-Marshal Souvang Zhu," Kiet said.

"Yes, him. They flew by when the bandits were just done pushing your car off the road. They shot them to death."

Ah, I am not altogether gross and disgusting, Kiet thought. I repel everyone because I am a ghost. "I must thank Marshal Zhu for avenging us so promptly."

"The radio says the bandits may be Rouge. Identification is difficult because they're riddled with too many bullets."

"And our bodies?"

"Ashes."

Unidentifiable cinders. How, then, was it learned that the Citroën contained the Cuban? Binh and Kiet, logically. Alberto Festerra? No, thank you. The radio report stank of a prescripted press release.

Quin was calmer, breathing easier, her head buried in the crook of his neck and a shoulder. Kiet looked around his back at Le. "Why was the Cuban in our automobile, please?"

She squinted at him, seeing an idiot. "How should I know? It was your car. You are the *gardien de la paix*."

"Mother," Quin said, raising her head. "Bamsan recovered Bao for us."

The old woman lowered her eyes and fell silent. Kiet remembered—or was he dreaming?—the night before last, Le placing a blanket on him. This was to be the extent of

her affection, he realized. This policeman who was doubtlessly violating her daughter. Grateful gestures made
while he slept. Wordless contrition.

"Madame Le," Kiet said evenly, "I was seeking the radio
version."

Quin answered for her mother. "You were giving him a
ride to Hickorn. No reason stated."

"Why would Captain Binh and I be doing that?" Kiet
wondered out loud.

"You weren't?"

"We were. It being common broadcast knowledge is the
peculiarity."

Quin hugged him and stood. "You couldn't be dead.
You're perfectly normal. You're talking in riddles."

"Like I did when I was alive?"

Quin kicked him gently in a shin.

"Death is perhaps not too bad," Kiet went on in exag-
gerated thoughtfulness. "I'd be done with paperwork. I'd
have no calls to return on telephones that do not work. No
criminals, no opium war mess, no—"

"Be serious," Quin scolded. She gave him a nonpunch to
the nose, hardly bending cartilage, and uncurled index
and middle fingers. "First Bao. Then you die. I can live
without those sorts of days. Two days, by the way. You
went to Obon for two days and didn't inform me."

"Sorry. A new development," Kiet said sheepishly.
"There was no time."

"Was the new development a famous Bamsan Kiet
hunch?"

"You know me too well."

"I know you as well as you let me know you."

A change of subject was in order, thank you. Kiet tilted
his head to the inner door.

"Yes, he is. We're staying with him around the clock. A
nurse friend of mine is in there. The doctors are cooperat-
ing too. This cubbyhole is what could be spared, but if I

149

have a word to say about it, we'll get the treatment facilities we have to have."

Kiet got up. "May I?"

"Bao doesn't know you've arisen from the dead. He would be appreciative," Quin said.

Kiet opened the door and peered in. Bao squatted on the floor, chest to knees, an upright fetal position. The nurse was kneeling beside him, dabbing perspiration from his forehead, soothing him with words Kiet could not hear. Kindness seemed to be the medication in their addiction treatment facility. Perhaps there were chemicals available too, but Kiet doubted if they would be much more effective.

Bao was trembling and perspiring heavily. With teeth clenched, he fixed on Kiet a tormented gaze not unlike those worn by the hospital people in the hallways. A major difference, though. He was not being haunted by the ghost of a deceased police superintendent. The anguish came from within.

Kiet took the boy by the shoulders, lifted him to his feet, and embraced him. Bao did not return his embrace, but when Kiet settled him down in his prior position, he smiled and said, "Man, you look like shit."

A comradely insult. Kiet left the room buoyant.

Quin said, "How did he react to you, Bamsan?"

"Bravely. He's a fine lad, you know. I think we've had a breakthrough, he and I."

"That's wonderful," she said, glowing.

"How long will he be, uh—"

"He's a relatively recent addict. The doctors think that's in his favor. His withdrawal period will be shorter. Only another day or two, we're hoping. The psychological addiction will be tougher to defeat. He won't soon be running with his musician friends, though. Because of the hepatitis, he'll be under supervised care for weeks."

Kiet nodded sympathetically.

"Are you going to be in Hickorn for a while?"

Under Le Canh's scrutiny, Kiet kissed her daughter chastely. "Yes, yes. If I leave again on a new development, Quin, I promise to notify you."

"You're going home to get some rest, aren't you?"

"Immediately following an intermediate stop."

"To where, should I ask?"

Kiet remembered a corny line repeatedly spoken by characters in the 1950s and 1960s American western dramas on Luongan television. "Dead men tell no tales."

Quin held her nose and said, "Get out of here and take a bath."

The dismantled Tess Twitch sandwich-board sign nailed over the Scarlet Mongoose's front door had been removed and renailed. Kiet instantly ascertained that the barrier had been disturbed. His clue was a slight refastening error.

Initially the back sides of the sign pieces—innocuously whitewashed plywood—faced outward. He could not guess why, but somebody had split the halves into quarters and tacked them up frontside out in a peculiar sequence. Tess Twitch's SEXsational pelvic region and legs were inverted on her upper body and beastly face. She looked to Kiet as if she had grown antlers; in his biased opinion, they beautified her.

The uniformed officer guarding the door saw Kiet and snapped to attention. He expressed relief and joy that his superintendent was alive, and said that Captain Binh was in the club. Kiet thanked the officer for his concern and asked him to reverse the Australian Amazon.

The officer pried off the sign slabs with an iron bar. Kiet said to refasten the plywood properly as soon as he was inside. He and Binh would henceforth come and go through the alley.

"And one trivial thing," he added. "Please do not advertise my resurrection, nor Captain Binh's. The nonlife of a ghost, I am learning, is fun."

151

Kiet located Binh at the main bar, sipping a Golden Tiger. He opened a bottle for Kiet, who took a pull, inhaled, and said, "The Scarlet Mongoose's aroma has not improved."

"You can shut it down, Superintendent, but you'll never in a month of Sundays get the stink out."

"Where is he?"

Binh pointed above and behind Kiet. "The mezzanine. The peep shows are up there."

"Excuse me?"

"I didn't know about them either. You feed in coins and watch a beaver flick."

Kiet knew without knowing why that Binh was not referring to a wildlife travelogue. His colloquialisms were maddening. "Did he object?"

"To the Scarlet Mongoose? No way. He's like a pig in mud. Superintendent, how did you know?"

"This revolutionary Communist agrarian specialist is a soft-skinned dandy who enjoys imperialistic luxuries. My first impression was KGB, but please allow me to renege. He does have a master other than Fidel and Fidel's masters, I'm certain. He betrayed his master. Or the master unilaterally betrayed him."

"The bottom line is that he's scared shitless," Binh said.

"Indeed. He is safe and there is food and liquor—did he get his Dunhills?"

"He's on his second pack. And correct me if I'm wrong. You're saying Festerra was in Zhu's cross hairs, not us?"

"Perhaps."

"Why?"

"Have you asked him?"

"I tried. He won't even shoot the breeze. The weather, soccer, girls. Zilch. He wouldn't say guano if he had a mouthful."

"He is comfortable?"

"You bet. Food, booze, smokes, and jack-off movies. What more could you ask for? He bitched because Vinnie didn't have Cuban rum, but he's making out real fine on Puerto Rican. He's drinking Cuba libres, Superintendent, and he's about half in the bag, so if you're going to jerk his chain, I'd strongly recommend going for it pretty soon, you know."

"I wonder if he and Little Big Vinnie Jones are friendly?"

"We're on the same wavelength, Superintendent. I whipped that on him sort of casually, you know. He said he wasn't, but once we got in here, he seemed to know where everything was."

"Mr. Jones threatened to 'bring heat' on us," Kiet said.

"Nothing yet," Binh said. "The uniforms guarding this dive haven't heard of any flak coming down from high places. Little Big Vinnie's keeping a low profile."

Kiet trudged the mezzanine stairs. Alberto Festerra was stooped over the viewing glass of a device that resembled an arcade computer game. The machine was not Pac Man or Space Invaders. Backlighted pink letters identified it as Crotch Cannibals. On an adjacent table was a rum bottle, an ice bucket, a glass, and several packages of cigarettes.

Kiet returned to Binh, who asked, "You didn't get anything that quickly, did you? You're good, but—"

"No. He didn't even see me."

"He's juiced, Superintendent. It could have been the right moment."

"No," Kiet said. "If he won't confide in us when he's frightened for his life, he won't when he's inebriated."

"What's his Achilles' heel, then?"

"Perhaps he will expose it and we'll know. In the meantime, Captain, go home. Wash your body and sleep."

Binh glanced at his watch. "The next guard shift is due in fifteen minutes. I'll brief them and be gone. And yourself?"

"To bath and bed also," Kiet said. Immediately following an intermediate stop, he did *not* say.

19

Bamsan Kiet lived on the corner of Avenue Che Guevara and Rue Willie Mosconi. His property was walled, therefore literally a villa, but the "villa" definition was exceedingly generous. Its builder was a French tax official in the service of the last governor-general. He was a middling clerk with pretensions, who believed he had erected a miniature estate by erecting two meters of concrete around it. The walls satisfied a second need—alleviation of paranoia. At the time, the early 1950s, the Vietminh were taking their complaints to the cities of Indochina. The tax man swaddled himself in cement, wrongly fearing that Hickorn colonials would be bombed and butchered.

Kiet's house itself was a cramped four rooms, extremely comfortable on the Luongan average, but scarcely an object of envy to the moneyed. So confining were the lot dimensions that the wall and the wrought-iron spikes atop it cast perpetual shadows on the ribbonlike grounds. This was Kiet's sole objection to the design; the absence of sunlight made a horticulture hobby impractical.

Kiet had lived at 590 Avenue Che Guevara since the

death of his beloved wife, Tien. Three times a week a maid shopped, did laundry, and cleaned house. Five years ago Kiet adopted a stray cat, an obese and arrogant animal of indeterminate age. It ate kitchen discards and came and went as it chose. In the monsoons it cried at the door like an abused infant and slept on its master's bed. In the dry season it was seldom seen. This domestic feline that purred and drooled on the laps of strangers like Ril Thoi treated Kiet like a flunky. Kiet punished the creature by refusing to name it.

Kiet had pondered his status before going home. His hesitancy was silly, he knew. He was, after all, deceased. A corpus delicti of gray residue inside a scorched hulk of a turbocharger-augmented, eight-Chevrolet-cylinder Citroën at the floor of a gully. If Hickorn radio said he was dead, he was *dead*. He would not be under surveillance. If anything, he would have been looted.

He was neither. His belongings had not been disturbed and there were no strange automobiles parked nearby. Kiet bathed, scrubbing himself until he tingled. Clad in only a robe, he went to the kitchen and removed from its carton the purchase made at his second "intermediate stop," the neighboring twenty-four-hour grocery.

He switched on the oven of his electric stove and looked fondly at dear, matronly Mrs. Smith's apple pie masterpiece. Just like on the carton photograph, a latticework of dough overlapped on the fruit-and-spice confection. He pictured Madame Smith as a chunky, change-of-life Caucasian lady with round florid cheeks and twinkling eyes, a grandmother of course, who was never without an apron and a smile.

Quin could not possibly disapprove. He had burned thousands and thousands of calories dodging .50 machine-gun bullets. And was the apple not a fruit, a natural food fabricated by the healthful triad of sun, water, and soil? Besides the vitamin and mineral benefit, the culinary experience would be culturally broadening. Kiet had never tasted an apple. He had some knowledge of the species, beginning at *lycée*, but the fruit was indigenous to temperate latitudes, essentially unknown in the tropical Kingdom of Luong.

Kiet slid the pie into the oven, feeling adventurous and scientific, strongly identifying with Vasco da Gama and Albert Schweitzer.

He slammed the oven shut and heard rapping on the front door. This was a rare instance when he wished he had acceded to Binh's nagging and carried a gun. He crept to a window by the door and peeked. The caller was not an intruder, not a fastidious assassin. It was Quin.

"Bao is sleeping," she said, coming in. "Mother is with him if he awakes."

"Is he better?"

"He's not worse. To me, at this stage, that's better."

"Does your mother know where you are?" said Kiet, a good host who kissed his guest and took her wrap. And her blouse.

"Unbutton it first, Bamsan," Quin said.

"Does she?"

Quin unfastened the sash of his robe. "Are you worried?"

"No," Kiet lied.

"I fibbed and told her I was going to the apartment to be certain everything was locked up and turned off. We left so suddenly I wasn't sure.

"I've done what I can for Bao. I've neglected my other man. We haven't a lot of extra time, Bamsan. Mother knows how long to the minute it takes to go from there to the apartment and back."

Quin spoke the second sentence en route to the bedroom, towing Kiet by his robe sash.

Later.

"Bamsan?"

"Quin?"

157

"Stop that, you lecher. Do you smell smoke?"

Oh, no, Kiet thought. His healthful triad rationalization fell apart. She would skin him if she knew he was planning to eat *any* pastry. He untangled himself from legs and linen, ran into the kitchen, removed the scorched pie from the oven, hurried outside, and flung it over the villa wall into the alleyway.

Quin was dressing. "Do we have a fire?"

"It was probably someone upwind burning garbage, blowing their smoke right into my kitchen. Very rude."

"It didn't smell like garbage. Come and fasten my bra. No, it smelled sweet and familiar. I smelled this once, a long time ago, at a feast after the funeral of a distant uncle. He was a very rich man. On the feast table were all kinds of imported delicacies. Apples! It smelled like apples."

Kiet regretfully rehooked her bra and asked, "Apples? What is an apple?"

20

"You must know the phoenix legend, Bosha," said Minister of Defense Cuong Van. "It has an Arabian origin. Every five hundred years the phoenix consumes itself by fire and a new, young phoenix springs from the ashes."

It was the following morning. Kiet, Binh, and Van were at the Scarlet Mongoose, drinking tea, seated on the edge of the stage where Tess Twitch danced out of her G-string. Kiet smiled and said, "But I am the same worn-out model, Cuong."

"Don't laugh, Bosha. You know how our astrologers and soothsayers are. They exploit anything that seems super-natural, any 'sign,' and claim they predicted it. Their business jumps. Many Luongans are superstitious and gullible. They believe those charlatans, and the sight of you two yesterday evening, head to toe in soot—particularly yourself, Bosha—was easy to extrapolate. My friends, you have arisen from the dead."

"Like Elvis," Binh said.

Cuong Van looked at him and then Kiet. "Regardless, I'm glad you sent a uniformed officer for me. I'm glad

159

you're the same worn-out Bosha, not dead or some mythical creature. I didn't know what to believe."

"Thank you, Cuong. Where opium is concerned, I don't believe anything or anybody," Kiet said. "Perhaps I shall lie low and remain dead for a while longer."

"To keep your enemies off balance? A good plan and I'll assist you any way I can. For starters, would you like me to do anything with Souvang Zhu?"

"Not yet," Kiet said. "I doubt that we can prove intent. Let him have his freedom. We'll see what he does with it."

"Lon Muoi?" Van said.

"Associate Deputy Minister of Defense for Drug Enforcement Investigation Lon Muoi. Why does his name come up now, Cuong?"

Cuong Van took from his pants pocket four small objects and gave them to Kiet. "A circular bug and the rectangular bug," Kiet said. "*And* a circular bug and a rectangular bug. Twins?"

Van nodded. "Your cynicism about Lon Muoi raised suspicions. It caused an itch that I scratched. Muoi is a bright boy, but he found the two bugs awfully fast. We brought in another man, an army captain and good soldier. His electronics background isn't as extensive as Muoi's. As you can see in your hand, he did a fine job."

"So Muoi knew you knew your office was bugged, sir," Binh said. "He swept it and coughed up two out of four. You're happy and he's still got you wired."

"That's logical," Van said, nodding.

Kiet described his bizarre cathedral rendezvous with Tip Taylor. "A computer virus too," Van said. "Muoi might be the one person in Hickorn with the expertise to sabotage the Americans' computer."

"Indeed," Kiet said.

"Why would he?" Van said.

"So he can neutralize the Ministry of Defense and throw a monkey wrench into the American drug enforcement program too, sir," Binh suggested. "Which could mean he's either self-employed or working with the Russkis or Little Big Vinnie."

Kiet related his cozy chat with Ambassador Shiherazade and Alberto Festerra, and his Obon adventure.

Cuong Van shook his head. "Shiherazade enlisting you as an ally? Our *lycée* chum Ril Thoi serving you chocolate and a Cuban? Can our opium war become any stranger?"

"Probably. By the way, Cuong, has Mr. Jones, the owner of this lovely establishment, taken the injustice of his closure to lofty places? He threatened to—" Kiet looked at Binh for the phraseology he had forgotten.

"That you would pay for this, Superintendent. That he had friends, who if you play chickenshit with me, Kiet, you're gonna be pounding a fucking beat. Please remember I am merely quoting."

"Splendid memory, Captain," Kiet said.

"The American gangster has substantial influence, the highest-quality influence money can buy." Van tugged an earlobe. "I never drift out of earshot where palace and National Assembly and ministry-level gossip is concerned. His Royal Highness's wisdom has blessed Luong with incredible stability, but you know as well as I, Bosha, that a coup d'état is only a cabal of colonels and a few tanks from actuality. I listen to everything and I have not heard the rustle of mobster money."

"A near-the-ground profile," Kiet said.

"Low profile, Superintendent."

"Why hasn't he carried through with his threat?" Van said. "Although I'm not personally acquainted with this Vincent Jones, I have been told by knowledgeable people that the Western organized criminal, the Mafioso, is extraordinarily vindictive. Nothing matters more to him than his twisted code of honor. He lives for the satisfaction of a vendetta."

"Perhaps Mr. Jones and Air Vice-Marshal Zhu are chummy," Kiet said as it occurred to him. "Perhaps business supersedes honor."

"I've never heard their names spoken together in a sentence of gossip, Bosha. That doesn't, however, prove they aren't associated. What about your Cuban? You say that he is at home in this putrid club."

"He could be a regular customer, Cuong, but I think the familiarity is deeper."

"Detaining him in an unauthorized location is probably illegal," Van said, his eyes smiling.

"How can we know? We are not lawyers," Kiet said.

"If we're real quiet we can hear him snoring," Binh said. "He's passed out on the couch in Vinnie's office. He polished off damn near a liter of Bacardi last night. He's got to have a monster hangover."

"He is a troubled man. Have you and Señor Festerra been properly introduced, Cuong?"

"No, Bosha. A discourteous oversight on your part."

"Forgive my manners," Kiet said, then glancing at Binh: "Captain, I wonder if he might care to join us. I have a hunch it is the ideal moment for a serious conversation."

Binh grinned broadly. "Leave it to me, gentlemen."

In the commotion of the raid and shutdown, the musicians had left their instruments behind. Binh chose deliberately, finally deciding on the cymbals that tolled Tess Twitch's anatomical feats. Bamsan Kiet and Cuong Van sipped their tea and listened to repeated clashings punctuated by moans and Spanish-language curses.

"Reveille," Van remarked.

"Little Big Vinnie's office walls are rather thin," Kiet said.

Binh brought out Festerra, who walked in jerky, mincing steps. Kiet performed proper introductions, offered a cup of tea that was declined, and said, "You appear brittle this lovely morning, Mr. Tropical Agriculture Expert."

"I have nothing to say, Kiet."

"On the contrary, señor, you shall have much to say. You insist we are responsible for your protection, yet you refuse to reveal information that might help us keep you

162

alive. You are terrified of virtually everyone. Your fear of Ambassador Shiherazade is especially baffling. He is, after all, your superior, your mentor, your master. And did he not express a desire that we pool our knowledge to defeat opium?"

"He is not my master."

"Sure," Binh said.

Festerra was chasing the Dunhill between his lips with a lighter. Kiet took the lighter from his trembling hand, lighted it for him, and said, "Very well, he is not your master. I accept that. You are partners, equals. Explain, please."

"I did not say that."

"Where does Mr. Jones fit in, please?"

"Who?"

Kiet groaned. "Bringing you here is the first luck I've had in this damnable opium war, señor. I would not have guessed you were in cahoots otherwise. Speak to me."

Festerra did not reply.

Kiet leaned toward Festerra and patted his forearm. "Listen to me, Alberto," he murmured. "For your sake, you must cooperate."

"Superintendent Kiet is right," Cuong Van said. "There are mixed opinions regarding your fate, the three of you. There is no consensus whether you are dead or alive."

Kiet caught his drift and recognized his cue, a mental synchronization borne of a lifelong friendship. "Captain Binh and myself have a civic duty to clarify our status. Since you were with us, Alberto, you shall be involved in the clarification."

"Clarification?" Festerra asked as he ground his cigarette out and reached for another.

Kiet lighted it. "Yes. We'll spend a glorious afternoon being conspicuously alive. A nice lunch downtown. French food, if you prefer. Or Chinese. Do you like yogurt and curry? We can dine Indian. You pick the café. Compliments of the Hickorn Police Department. Then a stroll.

163

Perhaps to the river. We'll eat early and have all this done before siesta. A quarter of Hickorn's citizens will observe us and babble the good news to the other three quarters."

"No," Festerra said.

"Oh, I understand that we will be at risk, but Minister Van is augmenting my patrolmen with troops."

Van sighed and said, "Superintendent Kiet, we will do our utmost, but we aren't infallible. As I've been attempting to tell you, a lone sniper—"

Kiet interrupted with a finger to his lips and a hiss. "He worries excessively, Alberto. Captain Binh and I are Hickorn's senior police officers and you are an esteemed visitor who is selflessly donating his services to opium eradication. The public deserves evidence that we are alive and well."

"No," Festerra said. "No."

"You have no faith, Alberto, that we are capable of protecting you?" Kiet whined, lowering his eyes to feign loss of face.

"You cannot do anything for me."

"We can do a lot for you," Van said.

Festerra spat on the floor.

Kiet slapped him. "Excuse me, señor, but when you speak to a Luongan by spitting, it is as if you are spitting in his face."

Although Kiet had not slapped him hard, his intent less an angry reaction to an insult than a jolt to the man's obstinacy, Festerra held his cheek as if it were bleeding. "I knew Hickorn policemen beat and tortured their prisoners."

"Stop it!" Kiet said. "Do you want to file a human rights violation complaint? Splendid. I'll even provide the appropriate printed form. But later. You have problems of a greater immediacy. I think your only solution is to depart Luong and either return home or seek political asylum. If the latter, to which nation, please?"

"Zhu shot down your car, Kiet. He can shoot down a plane."

"He will not shoot down a civilian aircraft," Van said. "I guarantee it. As minister of defense, I do have a few strings I can pull. We can board you on any commercial plane and have you out of the country before Zhu or anyone else is the wiser. To be doubly cautious, I'll assign troops to the RLAF apron, with orders to deny access to the Mustang pilots. We will fly you to Bangkok, Hong Kong, or Singapore and guard you until you transfer to the plane that will take you to your final destination, whichever country you so choose."

"Whichever country?" Festerra asked, looking at Van and then Kiet.

"Within reason," Kiet said. "To which nation, please?"

"Miami."

Van and Kiet exchanged shrugs. Kiet said, "I defer to my well-traveled adjutant."

"Miami is an American city in the southern tip of the state of Florida. It's less than a hundred miles from Cuba. Miami's population is heavily Hispanic."

"Ah," Kiet said. "The Russians are angry with you. The Luong Rouge are angry with you. And Fidel is angry with you. What on earth have you done?"

Festerra blew a smoke ring.

Kiet took Festerra's cigarette and squashed it in an ashtray. "We're all through with coyness, Alberto. Miami is an expensive fare. You have to pay. Either pay with information or we shall go out."

Binh patted a flat stomach and stood. "Yeah, let's do lunch, Superintendent. I can always eat."

"I give up," Festerra said, taking a cigarette from the pack. "You win. What do you want me to tell you?"

"One hundred percent of what you know. Start at the end. Miami. Why Miami?"

"I have friends and family there. Almost every Cuban has family and friends in Miami."

"Have you been to Miami before?"

"Yes. Once."

"That doesn't wash, Superintendent," Binh said. "You split from Cuba to escape Castro and his commie regime. You land in America, you're there for the duration. You don't commute."

"I was infiltrated in and out of Miami for a specific mission," Festerra told Kiet.

"Mother Goose time," Binh said. "Fairy Tale City."

"Captain," Kiet said. "Continue, please, señor."

"To recruit a powerful American Mafia gangster experienced in high-level drug dealing and send him to Hickorn to operate under the supervision of the Soviet ambassador and myself."

"Holy shit!" Binh said.

"On whose orders?" Kiet said.

"It was a request from our Soviet brothers in Havana."

"KGB?"

"I'm not important enough to know such details, but I wouldn't be surprised."

"What is your job, please? Besides tropical agriculture, of course."

"I serve the revolution in a variety of functions."

"A Renaissance Red," Binh said.

"Did your Soviet brothers explain the reason for their request?"

"In general terms, which you have already guessed. The Golden Triangle opium war was under way and the trade was diverting into Luong. Narcotics are destroying the resolve of the West. Cocaine from Latin America, heroin from Asia and the Near East. The opium war was perceived as an opportunity to gain control of the Golden Triangle opium trade through third parties, to maintain the flow, and to bring hard currencies into socialist economies ravaged by American imperialist greed."

"Your selection of Little Big Vinnie is enigmatic, Señor Festerra. Inscrutable. We are of the impression that Mr.

Jones is neither high level nor powerful. His very existence is precarious. That scorned daughter of the Cleveland godfather, Captain?"

"Cookie," Binh said. "He dumped the wrong broad."

Cookie, Kiet thought: leather jacket, pimpled complexion, bovine breasts.

"He came recommended by Miami crime figures and he was available," Festerra said.

"No," Kiet said. "I think not. Alberto, you are intelligent. You aren't the sort of fellow who makes such an absurd mistake. My stomach is rumbling, begging me for lunch. Talk to me, Alberto, or we shall go."

"Kiet, have you ever stood in a meat line with a ration card?"

"No."

"I have. Good commodities are not often to be had in Havana. When you can purchase them, you queue. It's a habit in Cuba to see a queue and join it. They may have something good and if you're fortunate, it won't be gone before your turn.

"There are no queues in Miami. There is no rationing of meat and other commodities dear to the palate and the senses. Soap, cigarettes, TV sets, leather shoes, rice, candy, on and on and on. You pay money and you can purchase the bounty of the world! I thought it was propaganda but I saw for myself when I infiltrated."

"You also saw the true potency of money," Kiet said.

"Yes. I earned a substantially higher wage than the average Cuban and I had sophisticated tastes, but all the pesos in Cuba are worthless if there are no products to spend them on."

"The Marxist-Leninist supply-and-demand curves," Binh said. "Sometimes they never cross. It's goofy."

"You were seduced by TV sets and lineless meat," Kiet said. "You deviated from the mission and intentionally recruited an incompetent and desperate American Mafia gangster opium trafficker. Little Big Vinnie doesn't work

167

for Havana or Shiherazade or Moscow or Fidel. He works for you, Alberto."

"Kiet, have you ever tasted an inch-thick top sirloin grilled over mesquite?"

"A life of mesquited sirloin lies before you, señor. A renewed mobster life in the happily forgiving hegemony of Cookie's Cleveland father lay ahead for Vinnie. The only requisite was shared wealth."

"Yes."

"What went awry?" Kiet asked. "Weren't you making your fortunes?"

"No, we were not. While Jones is not completely stupid, Kiet, he is vain and poorly motivated. He would rather be the big-shot club owner and man about town with the whores who dance on this stage. He traded trifling quantities of opium but had no interest in controlling the trade. I had to take total charge."

"Your visit to Obon?"

"Yes. Jones had resigned himself to secondary dealing. To *retail* dealing. My superiors were pressuring me for results. I had no choice but to go to the highlands to—what is the vernacular?—cop some weight."

"You got it," Binh said.

"Large quantities of narcotics, I presume," Kiet said. "What weights did Mr. Jones, uh, cop?"

Festerra smirked and looped an index finger. "A dribble."

"Not kilos?"

"No," Festerra said. "Grams and fractions of grams. He sold a little, gave away a little. He catered to his hangers-on and to entertainers who performed at other clubs on the Strip. His heroin connection and his generosity were the essence of his big-shot persona."

Bao Canh and Plutonium Gecko. No, they were not blameless. Yes, they could have purchased their drugs elsewhere. But why stray off and inconvenience yourself when Jones's ego made a transaction so simple? Kiet had miscalculated Little Big Vinnie's importance in the trade, though not his immorality.

"So you went north to buy heroin and you struck a deal?"

"Yes and no. I had an agreement, although there was no refined heroin on the market in the bulk I required. I negotiated for morphine base instead. Twenty kilos a week indefinitely."

"Why no heroin?"

"They dealt with a major client who preferred to refine base into heroin. They had gotten into a pattern of reducing gum to base and were not about to assume the risk and cost of a lab to appease me, a newcomer."

"The major client refined in Hickorn?"

"It would not have been too smart to ask that question, Kiet. My judgment is yes. Hickorn."

"Who was your highlands supplier?"

"A strange alliance," Festerra said, amusement curling the ends of his lips. "A Shan who had broken with his people and a Kuomintang who had done likewise. They were the leaders. Bitter enemies in the past and partners today. You did not have to be brilliant to see that they distrusted each other. The common soldiers in the camp were neither Shan nor Kuomintang. They were Laotian and Thai army deserters. Since the war, the highlands are teaming with newly allied marauders. Then Ril Thoi raided us."

"Rude and vulgar of him," Kiet said. "Why, please?"

"He told me that his scouts had recognized me. I dispute that. I think my sellers accidentally wandered into territory Chairman Thoi regarded as his and his alone."

"He imprisoned you," Kiet said. "A revolutionary socialist booted a comrade into a bamboo cage."

"You are enjoying this too much, Kiet," Festerra said, lighting his next cigarette himself. "He lectured me endlessly on dialectical materialism and the workers' struggle."

Ril does that, Kiet thought.

"*He* makes money selling opium," Festerra said, looking hard at Kiet.

Kiet again patted the Cuban's forearm. "I know, Alberto. I know. The rank gases of hypocrisy spin our planet."

"Did Confucius say that?" Festerra said.

"Yes," Kiet lied, unwilling to claim the fetid homily that had rolled off his lips in the excitement of disclosure. "You could not have a clue on the identity of the Hickorn major client, I suppose."

"Guesswork," Festerra said. "Zhu."

"Splendid guess," Kiet said. "Lon Muoi?"

"Similar guesswork, yes," Festerra said, inhaling smoke.

"Ambassador Shiherazade?"

"No."

"He frightens you because he has probably concluded that you and Vinnie were double-crossing him?"

"Yes. I don't think he was ever completely fooled. He became cool toward me after the kilo of heroin was found with the murdered hooligan. Shiherazade thought we were holding out on him. Maybe Jones was, but I had no knowledge of that kilo."

Kiet had planned to ask about Yung Lim, Jones's deceased thug with the kilo of Luong White No. 1 and the confiscated red Mazda RX-7 convertible that was to be the next automobile with which Binh would terrify his superintendent in the course of routine transportation. Apparently there would be no useful answers.

"You have done well, Alberto. A tiny addendum to our pact, please."

"We had a bargain, Kiet."

"A tiny tiny request," Kiet said.

Festerra sighed. "What?"

Kiet asked Van for the four bugs, then placed them in Festerra's shirt pocket.

"Transplant these for us, please."

21

"Superintendent, how did you know Festerra had electronics knowledge?" Binh asked.

Kiet, Binh, and an army corporal lifted from ministry guard duty and assigned the first eavesdropping shift were elbow to elbow on a bench in an unused storeroom above Lon Muoi's Ministry of Defense office. Cuong Van had donated the room, the soldier, and the radio that hung from a wall hook emitting roughly equal portions of static and bureaucratic gossip.

"He has soft hands and he is a variety of secret agent. While his revolutionary comrades are swinging machetes at sugarcane, Señor Festerra is snooping and playing volatile games," Kiet said. "Nowadays, electronic training is mandatory for secret agents. You can't spy effectively unless you can utilize voyeurism gadgets."

"Well, he sure installed the bugs and tuned them into the radio speakers fast," Binh said. "Three bugs scattered in Muoi's office, the fourth in his telephone. I'll bet it didn't take him ten minutes."

Nine minutes and twelve seconds, thought Kiet, who

171

had nervously timed the Cuban while scanning doorways. His anxiety had been groundless, for they had entered Lon Muoi's office at the height of siesta. There was not a person on the entire floor. Ministry employees were either at home snoozing or lazing in air-conditioned cafés. What was that splendid, Hollywood-filmed, 1950s motion picture? He remembered: *On the Beach*. Nuclear war radiation had killed nearly everyone but the movie's characters. Everywhere they went, there was nobody around. Like a Hickorn ministry during siesta.

Tropical agriculture whiz Alberto Festerra was meanwhile airborne over the South China Sea, en route to Bangkok. Then to Djakarta. Then an airplane change to a tour charter homeward bound to Los Angeles with Bali tourists. Then a Los Angeles–Miami nonstop on a commercial carrier. Kiet marveled at what Cuong Van could get done on short notice.

"Espionage is boring work," Kiet said. "Sitting on your butt for hours at a stretch, listening to banalities."

"Boring?" Binh said with an abbreviated headshake. The cramped storeroom encouraged economical motion. "No way. We're picking up some real juicy dirt."

Kiet stifled a rebuttal. Lon Muoi's postsiesta afternoon had consisted of colleagues streaming in and out of his office, squandering the remaining workday with gossip about salaries and marital infidelities. If that was not boring, he didn't know what was.

"Scandal, yes. Incriminating evidence, no," Kiet said. "That is my point."

"Well, I think it's great anyway," Binh said cheerfully. "In America you need a court order to wiretap. We just walked in and went for it."

"We'll be out of your way soon," Kiet told the corporal. "We aren't questioning your competence as a busybody. We are hoping our subject will say something stupid before long and give us something interesting to do."

"I'm happy for the company, sir, and I am not offended.

172

No, sir," said the corporal, who wore black leather belt and boots, starched dress whites, and helmet. "I'd be out in the heat, standing at parade rest, or in the barracks shining my boots and brass. No, sir, I'm happy for the relief."

"After what Festerra whipped on us, I'm superconfused about the Yung Lim rubout. I would've sworn on a stack of Bibles that Vinnie had had him whacked," Binh said.

Rubout, Kiet thought. Whacked. He said, "It certainly encourages us to analyze the killing from the opposite direction."

"You're saying you swallow Festerra's story?"

"Until we have evidence to support another theory, I'm not eliminating it."

"Do I take 'opposite direction' to mean that Yung Lim wasn't double-crossing Vinnie? He was loyal to Vinnie all along and had aced somebody else out of the kilo of smack?"

"Yes, you do."

"Lim was muscling into the big guys' operation on Vinnie's orders," Binh said. "Vinnie was bypassing Festerra and Shiherazade, figuring to move into the major leagues on his own. On the assumption that Zhu and Muoi are into opium up to their beady eyeballs, they put out the contract on Yung Lim."

"Very plausible, Captain."

"An alternative scenario, Superintendent. Festerra and Shiherazade, either-or, got wind of Vinnie's double cross and zotzed his number-one slime as a lesson."

"Zotzed," Kiet said. "I love the sound. Yes, your second scenario has merits, but I wonder if a third exists."

"How come?"

"Little Big Vinnie was too calm and poised when we visited him shortly after the murder. He is a pathological liar but not a professional actor. With Yung Lim deposited outside as a homicidal message, Vinnie should have displayed some fear. I discerned none."

173

"Well, yeah. Maybe Yung Lim had entrepreneurial ambitions of his—"

Kiet raised a hand. Festerra had wired the room bugs to one of the radio's stereophonic speakers, the telephone bug to the other. The telephone speaker was finally broadcasting intelligible noise. Previously, consistent with Hickorn's creaky telephone network, the sounds they had eavesdropped were busy signals and loud clicks segueing to utter silence, followed immediately by profanity and receiver slamming that resonated through the storeroom floor.

"Hey-y-y, muchacho!"

Muchacho? Spoken in a lilt reminiscent of Alberto Festerra's Spanish accent. Kiet looked at Binh, who lipped *z-h-u*.

Lon Muoi: How'd you get through, sir? The lines are worse than usual. A dial tone's a major miracle.

Souvang Zhu (chuckling): My good looks and personality, kiddo. Plus an airman who kept at it till he lucked into a free line. I don't make unreasonable demands of my boys, but when the airman said he reached you, I spared him the cigarette and blindfold.

(laughter)

Muoi: What's the latest?

Zhu: On the Three Stooges?

Muoi: Yeah.

Zhu: Now you see 'em, now you don't.

Muoi: Me too. The word on the streets is that Kiet has risen from the dead. Can you *believe* it? Sometimes I think Luong's in the Stone Age."

Zhu: Keep the faith, muchacho.

Muoi: You can count on me, sir.

Zhu: Taylor?

Muoi: Nary a peep.

Zhu: That's weird, but Tip doesn't have antennae worth a shit. The word on Festerra is that he's bye-bye.

Muoi: I thought you—

174

Zhu: Stop the music! The walls have ears.

Muoi: Not these hallowed walls. I'm the bugor. Old Man Van is the bugee. I faked the esteemed soccer hero out of his socks on the two bugs I [clears throat] removed from his office. Modern electronics in Luong is a telegraph key. Not to worry.

Zhu: All right. You know what you're doing.

Muoi: Festerra's where?

Zhu: Old Man Van has a gray matter cell or three flickering, bucko. People who owe me at Hickorn International said the gear was coming up on the plane before they knew what had happened. Festerra's head was shaved. He was in a saffron robe, in a cluster of monks going home to Bangkok. On the other hand, they could have been hallucinating and Festerra's really dead.

Muoi: But if Festerra's alive—

Zhu: Kiet and Binh are too.

Muoi: Unfortunately.

Zhu (laughing): They're saying Kiet grew wings. He was seen flapping his wings, flying out of a bonfire.

Muoi: Didn't you—

Zhu: Nobody could live through that. Maybe they jumped clear. Mellow out, champ. I'll handle him and the boy wonder if need be.

Muoi: Are we doing it? You said I was ready.

Zhu: That's why I called. A promise is a promise. Get your bod out here before sundown. We can do.

Muoi: (loud unintelligible exclamation)

Severed connection. Rapid movement. Muoi shouting that he was gone for the day.

Kiet and Binh took the back steps two at a time. The red Mazda RX-7 convertible was parked beside the alley door. They got into he car just as a silver BMW 318i sedan exited the ministry's alley-level parking garage.

"Slouch down, Superintendent. That's Muoi's Beamer."

Kiet fidgeted in his bucket seat and tried to retract head into upper body, though he was sure the retraction was

175

illusory, the result of hunching his shoulders upward. Why did Binh's favorite automobiles have to be space capsules?

"We're in luck. He's leaving the other way. How does that little son of a bitch rate?"

"Excuse me?"

"The ministry garage wasn't intended to be a garage, you know. They just knocked out some walls and reinforced some pillars. Parking in America is a status symbol when you don't have a lot of spaces at your workplace. You're assigned a slot, you're in. You've got it made."

Kiet suppressed a groan. Lon Muoi and his Beamwhatever were at the end of the alley, merging into street traffic. Escaping. And Binh was fretting about a perquisite. "Captain, perhaps he was illegally parked."

"Yeah, well."

"May we? Please."

"Oh. Right." Binh started the car and edged forward, frowning, saying "There's one consolation. He didn't have a chauffeur. That'd be superhard for me to deal with, that twit having a chauffeur. He's my age, you know."

"Yes," Kiet said, unhunching his shoulders.

"You know what?"

"No," Kiet said.

"It's his own car. Got to be. That explains why he's driving himself."

"His father is a wealthy rice wholesaler and miller," Kiet said.

"Yeah. Must be nice. You figure the airport, Superintendent?"

"Probably. He went that direction."

"We'll lay back, cool it. He'll make us if we follow too closely."

"Thank you."

To Kiet's astonishment, Binh indeed "cooled it." He drove at the pace dictated by traffic, neither yelling at obstacles, animate or inanimate, nor shortcutting via sidewalks. Quin would love this, Kiet thought, the blood

pressure and cholesterol aspects of automotive modera-
tion. Also, the convertible top was down and the airflow
was invigorating. A pleasant spin.

"They're staring at us, Superintendent."

"Who?"

"Ninety percent of the people we're encountering. Look
at those bulging eyeballs. It's that phoenix thing Minister
Van was saying. I was thinking ahead, anticipating this
problem, us being downtown at siesta wakeup in a conspicuously groovy set of wheels. Slip these on and slouch."

Binh grinned sinisterly and made an *O* with thumb and
forefinger. Kiet could not see his eyes inside the opaque
blue plastic. Furthermore, the wraparound sunglasses
made Binh appear reptilian. Kiet sighed and obeyed.
"Wonderful. They will never recognize us."

"Providing you really make an effort at slumping into
your seat, Superintendent. You're an extremely tall man.
Scrunching isn't going to hurt our incognito situation one
little bit, and if you ask me it isn't that gigantic an
imposition."

Slumping, slouching, scrunching. Binh was nagging
Kiet and he hated it. Really. He released his seat-belt
buckle. In an overpowered automobile featuring Binh at
the controls, that was akin to discarding your parachute in
a kamikaze plane. But freedom of movement faciliated
slumping, slouching, scrunching.

"Better?"

"Outstanding."

At the foot of Richard Nixon Boulevard, Kiet glanced at
his mirror and said, "Blow out some carbon, please."

"Huh? Are my ears plugged up? You're asking me to get
on it?"

Kiet refastened his belt and tightened the shoulder
harness. "With extreme reluctance. Peruse your mirrors,
Captain."

"Shit. Muoi's three cars back. How'd he get behind us?"

"Does it matter?"

177

"Nope, not at this point in time, I guess. Opening a lead on the Beamer is top priority. Hang on, Superintendent."

Kiet reflexively gripped his knees, a futile precaution, yes, but psychologically heartening. This maniacal run seemed longer and therefore at lower velocity than in the deceased Citroën, but they were tracking solidly and precisely, without the suicidal bucking and drifting of the turbocharged hot rod. When the Hickorn International terminal came into view, Kiet had released his kneecaps and was partially relaxed.

"A piece of cake," Kiet said, summoning the expression from a near-forgotten war movie enjoyed in a Hickorn cinema. John Wayne, the Duke, dispatching Japanese to their ancestors? Or was it David Niven, a Nazi-thwarting commando? He was not confident of the literal translation either, although he sensed an intimation of élan, the taunting of death.

"Yeah. No big deal," Binh said with a blasé shrug. "This puppy is a helluva road car. It sticks like glue and definitely hauls ass, but top-end torque kind of sucks when you compare it to the Citroën, you know."

Kiet concealed a smarting ego. He thought they had shared danger, thought they had mocked the Grim Reaper, had spit in his skull face. Instead they had shared tedium. He was glad he had resisted the thumbs-up salute. "Stop at this side of the terminal. We can look around the building and observe the RLAF hangar and apron, which is Muoi's likely destination."

"My very sentiments. Are you pissed at me, Superintendent? Your voice is funny."

"No."

Binh drove to the terminal corner and noted, "None too soon."

They got out and Kiet, whose eyes were older and not as keen, moved closer and confirmed what Binh had seen, Lon Muoi's BMW sedan approaching the Royal Luongan Air Force area.

"Five'll get you ten it's a big-time heroin transaction, Superintendent. You heard Muoi. He was like a little kid, he was so excited. My feeling is that Zhu's giving him more responsibility, more weight. It's some kind of watershed event for the twerp."

Kiet's intent silence told Binh to wait and see.

They watched Air Vice-Marshal Souvang Zhu hop down from the wing of a P-51 Mustang, raise both arms, and greet Associate Deputy Minister of Defense for Drug Enforcement Investigation Lon Muoi by slapping his upraised hands. Binh defined the peculiar rite to Kiet as "phony high-five shit." Muoi then climbed onto the Mustang wing and into the cockpit. Zhu mounted the wing and crouched beside Muoi.

"What the hell is going on?" Binh asked.

Zhu, resplendently grubby in jeans and T-shirt, was playing the boastful café aviator, swooping and dipping flattened palms. Kiet shook his head.

"Where's the heroin?" Binh said. "Dope's in the equation. Has to be."

Zhu jumped off the wing, stepped back, and twirled a finger. Muoi started the Mustang engine and taxied to the runway.

"I fear Minister Muoi's childlike excitement is unrelated to opium," Kiet said. "His momentary flying career with Royal Air Luong?"

"Yeah. That's right. He groundlooped their flagship DC-3 and totaled it. They canned him. Oh, no! Are you thinking what I'm thinking?"

"Flying lessons," Kiet said. "Lon Muoi's first solo in Zhu's fighter."

Binh's obscenity was smothered by the full-throttle Mustang engine. Muoi's takeoff was not pretty—snaking when the tail lifted, one wheel breaking ground before the other—but nobody was going to die. He circled the airport once and landed at the midpoint, touching down fast, bouncing and ballooning, bouncing and ballooning,

bouncing and ballooning. Gray puffs wafted from the wheels, as if primitive smoke signals. The P-51 turned off at the far boundary. Muoi taxied to the RLAF ramp and a congratulatory repetition of Binh's ridiculed high-fives.

"He didn't have fifty meters of runway in front of him," Binh said. "He's lucky. He should've rolled off into the swamp and flipped upside down."

"Were you wishing, Captain?"

"Yeah. Crash and burn was my preference, but you can't have everything. Don't tell me you'd go into mourning, Superintendent."

"No comment," Kiet said.

"I suppose they'll boogie into town and celebrate."

"Probably."

"So where does that leave us?"

"With a slight information increase," Kiet said.

"Speaking of wishful thinking. C'mon, Superintendent. Nice try, but we came up zilch."

"The briefcase," Kiet said.

"Huh?"

"Did your attention stray from the flight?"

"No way. I wasn't about to miss a fireball. Being a ghoul is fun. You're going to tell me yours did, aren't you? What briefcase?"

"The briefcase Zhu removed from Muoi's car and put behind the seat of that Mustang."

"Which Mustang?"

"The Mustang Marshal Zhu just boarded. The Mustang whose propeller is beginning to rotate."

22

It is said that in Southeast Asia the dry seasons are a little hotter than the rainy seasons, which are a little damper than the dry seasons. In Luong's meteorological case, this is a cynical misconception. The lowlands in and around Hickorn are not climatologically uniform. A distinct dry season parches, as it does now. A weeklong transition season follows. Then comes the southwest monsoon. Charged by the Bay of Bengal, rain falls twenty to thirty minutes per day, flooding paddies (good) and streets (bad). So violent are the downpours that ancient animist cults worshiped the phenomenon. But there *are* exceptions, weather anomalies.

Such an anomaly occurred while Kiet and Binh watched Zhu and his Mustang fighter disappear on the eastern horizon. They had debated trailing Muoi or staying until Zhu returned. The sight of Zhu steering eastward at low altitude ended the debate. Laos or Thailand, Kiet had said. Smack dab on the deck, underneath the radar, Binh had said.

The cloud had sneaked in behind the detectives. It was

the hue of iron and too high to eclipse the setting sun. Its timing and path was flawlessly treacherous. The wind against their backs was their warning, a very short fuse. Despite no experience at raising the Mazda's convertible top, Binh responded admirably and had the cloth roof in position within a minute.

But an automobile interior exposed one minute to a tropical drenching was analogous to one minute of ruptured water pipe. The cloud floated onward, an animist prankster. Binh went off, disguised in his wraparound sunglasses, and brought back an armload of towels. They mopped out the carpeting and seats, got inside and waited.

"Talk to me about opium chemistry, please," Kiet said.

"Well," Binh said, "in my District of Columbia year, we never busted a lab. They're rare in the Western destination countries. Golden Crescent heroin—that of Pakistan, Afghanistan, and Iran—is cooked in Europe. Golden Triangle dope, as we are painfully aware, is—was—cooked at the origin. I did have the opportunity to attend an informative DEA seminar for city police—"

"Cooked?"

"Refined, you know, from opium gum to morphine base to the heroin that's cut and sold on the street."

"We can presume that opium gum is reduced to morphine base in the highlands," Kiet said. "We know that it is not a difficult process and that it reduces the raw opium bulk at a ten-to-one ratio."

"Yep," Binh said. "You just add a precipitating agent and press out the liquid. The solid particulate is the base."

"Not difficult," Kiet repeated.

"Nope," Binh said. "Any moron who's had a day's training can do."

"The final cooking to heroin is increasingly complex?"

"You don't have to be a rocket scientist," Binh said, "but it's trickier. In terms of weight and volume, morphine base to heroin is one to one. Purity's the thing. A good chemist

182

will cook junk eighty-five to ninety percent pure; a mediocre cook less so. When you're smuggling, that's important. Your mule can haul more zing at less risk."

"Mule?"

"The scumsucker actually transporting the junk from point A to point B."

"Mule," Kiet said. "Of course. Are you familiar with the chemical cooking procedure?"

"Uh-huh. You treat base by drying it and mixing it with a solvent. Acetic anhydride mostly. Purify it through charcoal and, bingo, you're in business."

"How elaborate need the laboratory be?"

"We aren't talking any biggie, Superintendent. Pots and pans, heat lamps, water, waste removal. No sweat."

"Charcoal?" Kiet asked. "Like the charcoal we traveled with?"

"A finer grade."

"Readily available, yes?"

"Anywhere."

"The acetic what?"

"Acetic anhydride. An industrial chemical used chiefly in the manufacture of synthetic fibers, weed killers, film, and various plastics. You wouldn't ship it into Hickorn by that name. You'd ship on a phony manifest, which they did unless they were complete idiots. We'd never be able to trace it."

"Film?"

"Photographic film."

"What measures must be taken to conceal such a laboratory?"

"Waste discharge. Direct access to a sewer. You can't be dumping drums of the stuff somewhere. Odor, I'd say, is the major security problem."

"What smells?"

"The acetic anhydride. It's real pungent. We got to sniff a sample at that seminar. I can't exactly describe it to you. Vinegar, sort of, I guess."

"Requiring a sophisticated exhaust system, I suppose."

"Yeah," Binh said. "Either that or cook your poison in the boondocks."

Night had come and Kiet hadn't noticed. He pointed to lights low in the east.

"Zhu," Binh said. "Blinkers on each wing and the vertical fin. It sure ain't the Three Wise Men."

"How long has he been gone?"

"An hour, but it seems longer, doesn't it?"

"Indeed. How fast is his airplane, Captain?"

"A Mustang'll max out at four hundred miles per hour. At a sensible altitude, you know. You don't go full bore if you're brushing treetops. No way. Two-fifty's a whole bunch safer on the deck, and you're not exactly growing cobwebs either."

"Subtracting for a quick visit on the ground, Zhu's radius was one hundred miles." Kiet groaned. "One hundred and sixty kilometers."

"Farther than Chiang Mai. Halfway to Vientiane. He could've hacked a left and bopped into China too, Superintendent. The Western authorities turn a blind eye on China where opium is concerned. But who knows?"

"The terrain in Zhu's radius is rough. Would he chance landing on an unimproved airstrip?"

"He scooted out of here before sundown," Binh said. "He had so-so light. His buyers could set kerosene pots out for him. And don't forget, Superintendent, as much I hate to admit it, Zhu's a superhot pilot."

"No argument," Kiet muttered.

"Look, his gear is coming down. He'll be landing. Are we going to hang around and follow him?"

"No," Kiet said. "Muoi's briefcase will be empty and we are nearly positive what he has done, if not where he has been. And he is more alert than the boy minister. I question whether we could successfully trail him in a red convertible."

"Yeah, you're right. He'd make us in a second." Binh

started the car. Thanks to reverse gear and a heavy foot, tires clawed gravel, which pinged the floorboards. On Richard Nixon Boulevard, he added, "Home?"

"No. Your chemistry presentation was excellent, but I would enjoy a postgraduate course."

Binh laughed and said, "From the dean of Hickorn's heroin lab?"

"Yes, but since we lack a college catalog and the dean's identity, we should settle for next best."

"Huh?"

"Someone with alleged credentials."

"Our phony-baloney Mafioso?"

"Yes."

Binh shook his head. "What a letdown he was. What a goddamned jerk. Little Big Vinnie comes on like a made guy and he's hustling dime bags to kids."

"It has been too long," Kiet said.

"Yeah," Binh said. "I miss him too."

23

Vincent "Little Big Vinnie" Jones was a Hickorn home-owner, a recent purchaser of a Riverview Estates penthouse. Situated a kilometer south of the Strip on Ma San Boulevard, Riverview Estates had almost as recently leapt from slum to upscale chic. The building formerly served boatmen and barge crews, providing daily and weekly room rentals at cheap prices.

Opium money had impelled an ownership changeover and a major face-lift. Holes were knocked out of the walls separating the cubicle-size rooms and arched doorways were framed in. Painters and carpetlayers swept in immediately thereafter, completing the transformation from tenement warrens to five- and six-room luxury units.

To Kiet's understanding, a river view was the enticement. Moneyed homebuyers prized view property and paid thousands and thousands of dollars or yen or francs or pounds for houses that overlooked something. Anything. And Hickorn's flatness made view property extremely dear.

Kiet wondered if buyers could negotiate prices downward because of the smell, which was no enticement to him. Hickorn's inadequate sewage system discharged raw effluvium not far southward. Kiet asked Binh about bargain possibilities, and was sorry he had. Binh did not reply, he delivered a sermon.

He said that he was thoroughly disgusted with how they'd schlocked Riverview Estates; the same development group that had renovated the Double Happiness shopping arcade with excellence coming out of their ears, a class act, had inexplicably shamed themselves. Riverview was a different ball game. Condominiumized on a shoestring, humping the fast buck. Californication is what we're talking about, Superintendent, and it sucks; a boomtown climate is what we're stuck with and the bastards can reel in whatever the traffic will bear, which is a ton of bucks.

Kiet did not respond. Binh's oration could stand as is, thank you. They climbed an outer stairwell to the second-floor balcony, the penthouse landing. It was fenced by a rickety wrought-iron railing and covered with prickly green carpeting that Binh defined with a non sequitur as indoor-outdoor.

Binh unsnapped his patent leather holster, withdrew a nickel-plated, pearl-handled, Colt .45 automatic, cocked the hammer, and gave Little Big Vinnie's door a back-handed knuckle rap.

Binh loved his weapon a bit too much, Kiet thought. He said, "Captain."

"I'm not overreacting, Superintendent. The lights are out. He could be laying for us. Vinnie's penny ante, yeah. We can't forget he's mob. They're cobras, you know."

Binh knocked again, harder. No answer.

"He might be playing possum," he said, shaking the doorknob. "Look at this el cheapo door. Laminated hollowcore. I could jimmy this guy in a millisecond with plastic."

"Plastic?"

"A credit card. Slip it into the jamb and you're in."

"Of course."

A third pounding. Again, no answer.

"Wouldn't breaking the door down be more fun?" Kiet asked.

Binh smiled, said "Right on," and kicked it open. He jerked aside, avoiding the fusillade that wasn't, then dashed in, both hands around the Colt, waving it side to side like a wand. The unarmed Kiet entered and switched on lights.

"Mr. Jones is out for the evening." he said.

"I would be too," Binh said, scanning the living room. "Christ, this is tacky. Orange wall-to-wall carpeting. Cardboard furniture. A phony fireplace with a fake plastic log in it. God! Where does he think he is? Look at the painting above the mantel. It's gross beyond human comprehension."

Kiet looked. The painting depicted a springing tiger. The medium was phosphorescent pigment on a black velvet background. The piece was strikingly vivid and accurately drawn. So where was the artistic merit in Binh's criticism?

Before he could ask, Binh had begun his detective's preliminary sweep, narrating on the general disarray of the unit, and on the plastic and metal table and chairs in the dining area, contemptuously classifying the furniture style as Early Cold War. The kitchen was junk too, that garbage disposal and microwave oven a cheap trick to fool you into signing your life away for gadgets that will fall apart the third time you use them. Goddamn opium money, Superintendent, is blowing this schlock into Hickorn like the storm that inundated us at the airport. No difference, none, and that's not right, no way.

Binh came to what he thought was the bedroom, ceased his editorial, walked in, paused, and stumbled backward, hands raised across his face.

Kiet rushed to his adjutant, fearing he had been struck.

Then he smelled it too, a clinging rankness he unfortunately recognized. He spun 180 degrees, gagged, and pinched his nose.

Binh said, "We're not talking about an aroma from Old Man River here."

"Little Big Vinnie?"

"Couldn't see, but here goes." Binh inhaled, puffed his cheeks like an exotic aquarium fish, and plunged into the stench.

Kiet, in the meantime, opened every window and removed the splintered door from its hinges.

Fifteen minutes passed. Binh joined him on the riverview balcony, panting. "Held my breath three minutes. World and. Olympic record. I'll bet. Long enough. To see. What there was to see. Lo and behold. Holding a sawed-off. Twelve-gauge shotgun. Bet you a month's pay it's the goodie. That whacked-out Yung Lim. You thought the other shoe was gonna drop, Little Big Vinnie raising holy hell. Scarlet Mongoose closing. It's been two, three days. Smells like. He may have been zotzed. The night we. Padlocked him."

"Presumably," Kiet said. "Mr. Jones was *holding* the shotgun?"

"As in suicide? Nah. That's what they were going for, but they put the gun in his wrong hand. They were in a hurry, a superhurry, is how I read that screw-up. The entrance wound is in the right rear of the head, exiting the left front. Are you visualizing this, Superintendent?"

"Oh, yes," Kiet said.

"Well, they closed his trigger finger on the trigger. Fine so far, okay?"

"Yes."

"Except that the gun's in his *left* hand. Little Big Vinnie'd have to be a contortionist to blast himself in the right rear of his pointy head. Breathe fresh air for a minute, Superintendent, and I'll take you in and show—"

"No," Kiet said. "No. Unnecessary. I am visualizing perfectly."

"Any fresh theories to add to our list?"

"The heroin laboratory is the center of our universe, Captain," Kiet said. "The operators control Golden Triangle heroin. They are giving us headaches. They are responsible for us being on this balcony, in darkness, on duty when we should be with loved ones, not nauseated by the decomposition of an American gangster. They are destroying Luong and they are stealing our leisure time, Captain, yours and mine. Never mind. Disregard my self-pity. I apologize. What is important is this: An outsider learning the laboratory location is a threat to them."

"Are you okay, Superintendent?"

"I am. A kilo of Luong White Number One was in the late Yung Lim's possession."

"I'm still with you."

"Perhaps Yung Lim had discovered the laboratory and made a purchase."

"I'll buy that."

"Perhaps Lim revealed the location to Little Big Vinnie, who subsequently had him zotzed."

"When did he reveal the location?"

"Not long before his zotzing."

Binh snapped his fingers. "Vinnie wasn't surprised when we laid the bad news on him because Yung Lim had probably just been to the Scarlet Mongoose, probably in Vinnie's office so as to be inconspicuous. Vinnie had another goon waiting in the wings."

"Plausible."

"Yeah. Very plausible. These Mafia types, I'm telling you, you can't trust them, not even their own mothers can. Maybe Lim was pushing Vinnie, saying that since he had a pipeline to the lab, he deserved to be a full partner, him and Vinnie double-crossing the rival factions."

"Splendid. A double killer to apprehend."

"Yeah, well, I searched the bedroom, but I came up dry.

191

Knock me over with a feather, but Vinnie had porn and a package of French ticklers, party time for him and Tess Twitch. He'd built a Mickey Mouse hidden compartment in the bottom of a dresser drawer, where he's stashed cash, a dozen dime bags, and some miscellaneous crap. I'll order a forensic team out first thing in the morning, but it might be profitable for us to toss the rest of the unit now, you know."

Kiet hesitantly agreed. They searched systematically. The result, in Binh's words, was zilch *and* zip. The sole article of interest was an unread newspaper that had been delivered through a slot beside the door.

It was today's the *Hickorn Enquiring Mind*, a paper blatantly imitative of Western tabloids. It appealed to the superstitious and the suggestible, a readership that would unquestionably include Cuong Van's scorched-phoenix believers. The *Mind*, as it was known, a dismaying misnomer in Kiet's opinion, was Hickorn's second-best-selling newspaper.

Kiet looked at the front page and groaned. On the left was a photograph of a gyrating Elvis Presley, guitar strapped over a tight and glittery jumpsuit, belting out timeless lyrics. In the center was a crude drawing of a flying saucer, a Frisbee with taillights. On the right was a photograph of Bamsan Kiet, Hickorn's Superintendent of Police.

Kiet tossed it aside without reading the story. Binh grabbed the *Mind* before it fluttered over the balcony and said, "We're famous, Superintendent! They have reputable witnesses who saw us being beamed up from the Citroën a blink of the eye prior to contact with the riverbed and the explosion. This is garbage, but, what the hell, it's kind of fun, you know, and they even spelled my name right. I didn't rate a picture, but with the UFO and you and Elvis, there wasn't—"

"Why is Elvis on our spaceship, please? I do not remember Elvis being in the Citroën. Alberto Festerra yes, Elvis no."

"Pizzazz," Binh said, shrugging. "No other reason. Next issue, I'll bet we'll be having an exclusive interview with him. Us being detectives, the king's bound to reveal how come he's on an UFO."

"Doubtlessly," Kiet said. "The lack of evidence here is disappointing."

"We ransacked the dump," Binh said, shrugging again.

"The miscellaneous crap in his secret compartment?"

"Nothing really special," Binh said.

At Kiet's request, Binh went inside and retrieved the miscellaneous crap anyway. He gave Kiet a passport, an Ohio driver's license, a sepia photo of a mustachioed woman who was either Vinnie's mother or Cookie, and a strip of paper with a five-digit number and boxes printed under days of the week.

"Peculiar," Kiet said. "What is it and why the daily boxes?"

"It's common in America, Superintendent. You drop off dry cleaning or film. They tear a stub like this and give it to you. The other part of the ticket is retained by the merchant. It has the same number. The day your cleaning or pictures are to be ready is marked in the appropriate square."

"Why is no daily box checked?" Kiet said.

Binh shook his head.

"Shouldn't there be a company name on the slip?"

"In the States, there'd have to be. Hickorn's different. A laundry knows its customers. You whip a numbered slip on somebody, he'll regard it as impersonal, an insult. He'll lose face and take his business elsewhere."

"It isn't American," Kiet said. "The days of the week are in Luongan."

"One company in Hickorn that I know of is using the system. They do a heavy tourist trade. The photo-processing outfit in the Double Happiness arcade."

193

"Ah," Kiet said.

"Superintendent, excuse me, why are your nostrils twitching? Is the smell getting to you?"

"Yes," Kiet said. "A smell I cannot smell. A photographic chemical smell."

24

Kiet noticed that patrons of the Double Happiness arcade were not noticing Binh or himself.

"Well-dressed foreigners and Luongans are clogging the plaza and the expensive shops," he said. "Hundreds of people, and they're oblivious to two men who arose from the dead."

"They don't follow rumors that don't have the potential to fatten their wallets, and they don't read trash tabloids, Superintendent. They read financial journals. They wouldn't care about us if they had seen that *Mind*. They're too busy making money."

"It's ten o'clock at night. What are they all doing here?"

"Spending, Superintendent. Spending. If you got it, flaunt it."

Kiet and Binh walked to the side of the fountain closest to Double Happiness Photo. They spoke softly, the sound of cascading water ensuring privacy.

"Despite it being a while since the DEA seminar, the odor's familiar," Binh said, sniffing. "Other chemicals are masking, but acetic anhydride is definitely in the air."

"The second concealment requirement is waste discharge, yes?"

"No sweat. The developers went first cabin when they upscaled Double Happiness. They tore out the old sewer pipe and laid new. Hickorn Sewage Number Two Doo-doo and Chanel Number Five are not compatible fragrances."

"The photo lab isn't doing the volume business its neighbors are," Kiet said. "In fact, I haven't seen one person go in and I do not see a clerk at the counter."

"Well, if you're right, Superintendent, their clientele is real specialized. They sure as hell aren't gonna encourage the shutterbug set. Do you figure that's how Lon Muoi fell behind us after he split from the ministry with the lead he had? He made a quick stop for Zhu's you-know-what?"

"Indeed."

"What say we have us a little raiding party?"

"No. We might catch a cook and seize a kilo or two of heroin, but the laboratory will merely relocate."

"Maybe Lon Muoi's inside cooking his little heart out."

"I doubt it," Kiet said. "Lon Muoi dirtying his hands? No, thank you."

"Yeah. Makes sense. So maybe we ought to invite the twerp to the party."

"Splendid idea," Kiet said, suddenly inspired by an idea of his own.

He took two 100-zin coins from his pocket, gave one to Binh, and said, "At this late hour, the odds of a pay telephone granting us a line are exceptional."

"Yeah," Binh said, nodding in agreement. "If I were making book, I'd lay three to one, which for Hickorn ain't too shabby. We're ringing the guest of honor, right. Who else?"

"Headquarters," Kiet said. "Please notify whoever is on desk sergeant duty to dispatch officers to stand by across the street for our signal, on the pathway on the opposite side of the cathedral."

"Consider it done. I guess you'll be placing the crucial call. Know where to reach him?"

"At his family villa. Hopefully."

"Yeah, he still lives with Mommy and Daddy, doesn't he? The rice wholesaling and milling business must be super. The Muois have about the ritziest pad in the International District."

"Before we begin, tutor me on the slang term for adulterating heroin with the purpose of reducing its strength in order to increase profits."

"Stepping on it. Cutting it. They usually cut with milk sugar or an Italian baby laxative."

Drug addiction as a constipation cure? "And generic slang for the narcotic, please."

"Junk, shit, smack, h, horse, skag—"

"Sufficient, thank you. Shall we?"

Kiet and Binh dialed at adjacent kiosks. A servant answered Kiet: "Muoi residence."

Kiet, speaking through curled fingers to disguise his voice, asked for Associate Deputy Minister Muoi.

"Yes."

"They're cutting this batch," Kiet said, attempting a George Raft-Humphrey Bogart growl gleaned from film noir cinema.

Silence.

"You listening?"

"I heard you," Muoi said. "You sound like you're in a tunnel. Who is this?"

"A friend."

Silence.

"I ain't got all day."

"You're pestering the wrong person. I don't understand a word you're saying."

"Yeah, you do. You're stiffing me. This tip oughta be worth plenty."

"What tip? Batch? What are you referring to?"

"They're stepping on it."

197

"Stepping?"

"Don't play dumb, Muoi. They're stepping on your snack."

"Snack? You confuse me with a restaurateur."

Wretched, damnable slang, Kiet thought. He said in his best Bogie snarl, "Smack, punk. Smack. Clean the wax outta your ears."

"Who is the culprit in this riddle?"

"The cook. Cooks. Who do you think, stupid?"

"You're slandering a substantial person."

"Not interested, huh?"

"How can I be interested in a deranged puzzle?"

"Fifty percent, Muoi. Half for them, half for you. They're cheating your buyers too, dummy. So who do you think'll have to pay? With money and his life."

Kiet hung up. Binh was finished also.

"Superintendent, you were great! You came off like a genuine hood. He has to be scared shitless."

"Thank you."

"Everything's copacetic on my end. Four guys we can depend on big time will be you-know-where in twenty minutes. Where are we staking out?"

"I respect your judgment."

"What's the matter with your voice?"

"Growling and snarling are unnatural Luongan language tones. Are throat lozenges sold at Double Happiness?"

25

Twenty-three tenants in Double Happiness, and none was a pharmacy. Although Bamsan Kiet was denied conventional sore-throat medication, a tastier substitute became available via a union of detective tactics and luck.

The shop offering the farthest, straight-line view of Double Happiness Photo was Hickorn Chocolate Depot, a treasure trove of chocolate creams, chocolate truffles, chocolate cakes, chocolate toppings, chocolate figurines, chocolate mints, and chocolate logs. The French colonials, addicted to confections as they were, had not envisioned for Hickorn a shrine devoted exclusively to the fruit of the cacao tree. In retrospect, Kiet found this omission amazing.

Affluent arcade customers may have been oblivious to the Kiet-Binh-Festerra phoenixlike resurrection, but Hickorn Chocolate Depot employees—three comely young women—were not. They were also devoted *Hickorn Enquiring Mind* readers, who cooed and giggled and implored Captain Binh to autograph copies. He gallantly complied despite the urgency of surveillance and the fact that the adjutant was mentioned only once in the lurid story, on an inside column hemmed in by advertising for prayer cloths and padded lingerie.

Kiet was not in the least miffed that he, the front-page star, was virtually ignored. The snub was understandable in these circumstances, in which hormone release was palpable. Binh was also exuding charm, embellishing the *Mind*'s science fiction, establishing sexual friendships. Let him enjoy for a moment, Kiet mused; I am quite capable of monitoring Double Happiness Photo alone, thank you.

Binh's friskiness made him think of Quin and the artifice of seduction. It was a game they both relished, playing it as if they had just then met. The energy, the excitement. He had a sudden yearning for her so powerful it bordered on painful.

This store, however, was a consoling influence. The atmosphere was so dense with cocoa and sweet liqueurs, it seemed viscous. Inhalations of calorie-rich air anesthetized his ache, and donations of fruit- and nut-filled samplers by employees at the request of the dashing Binh soothed his scratchy throat.

After several minutes, Kiet began to resent Binh's distraction. Enough was enough. He was on duty. A breakthrough was in the offing. And how could any normal man remain vigilant throughout four-sided verbal foreplay? But to Kiet's acute embarrassment it was Binh who spotted Lon Muoi first.

He abandoned the ladies with profuse apologies and hand kisses, and hurried to Kiet, who had focused on the side entrance nearest Double Happiness Photo. He did not see Muoi until Binh reacted, because their quarry had, surprisingly, entered the main plaza from Avenue Dwight Eisenhower, through sliding doors that ostentatiously opened and closed by themselves.

"Jesus, Superintendent, he acts like he owns the place," Binh whispered.

Kiet was sucking on a papaya-and-macadamia-nut

200

cream, while holding for future medication a foil-wrapped chocolate bar the size and heft of a patrolman's baton. "Puhapsuhnzaplus."

"Huh?"

Kiet swallowed the delicacy and licked his lips. "I said that if our suspicions are correct, he perhaps does own the place."

"Yeah, you're probably right. He could afford to buy Double Happiness and have change to spare. Look at him strut, Superintendent."

Kiet looked, kneeling with Binh between glass shelving, the upper containing gift boxes of milk chocolates, the lower dark-chocolate tigers, their nakedness cellophaned. Those splendid cats, Kiet thought; they weigh a kilo if they weigh a gram.

"Disgusting," Binh added.

Kiet nodded, observing a weak and lazy boy. Slack rather than obese. Trace of a smirk. Upturned nose. Razor-cut hair, petrified with aerosol spray. Sandals, dark trousers, white shirt—the uniform of tropical commerce. Muoi's clothing was deceptively nondescript. Every article in his wardrobe was handmade in Hong Kong.

"We've got to say this for him, he's exercising some major-league cool."

"We do?"

"You know, prancing around like he just bopped in to buy a necktie. See, he's saying hello to someone. He just waved to this other geek. You'd think he was running for office. I gotta give him credit for balls I didn't think he had."

"Major-league cool," Kiet said, finally translating.

"Yeah. Say, you know, do you think I was coming on too strong with the foxes?"

Peculiar timing for a father-and-son chat, Kiet thought, eyes fixed on Muoi, who was too congenial and aimless to be believed.

"Well, do you, Superintendent?"

201

"Oh, no."

"I usually don't b.s. them. I don't have to, you know. They're bright girls too. They don't automatically gobble up every stupid word in the tabloids, you know."

"I know," Kiet said.

"They like to be teased."

"Yes." The glad-hand act of Lon Muoi, the substantial person, the acquaintance of many, seemed to be drifting toward Double Happiness Photo.

"Tantalized, you know. They asked me about Elvis, why we were all there and what he was like."

"Where?"

"On the flying saucer."

"Of course." Muoi was alone, window browsing, casually working his way to Double Happiness Photo.

"I said that Elvis was a neat guy. I said that he was responsible for talking the aliens into rescuing us when the Citroën plunged over the cliff. I said he was their guest. They helped him contrive his death. He was sick of being in a fishbowl. I said that Elvis and the aliens didn't talk much. Elvis sang to them and they listened. I said he sang 'Heartbreak Hotel' and 'Blue Hawaii' while we were aboard."

Kiet groaned. "While *we* were aboard?"

"I was just kind of following the story line. Good clean fun, you know. Like I said, they don't actually believe that hogwash, but they don't exactly disbelieve. They're country girls, you know, bright, but not real sophisticated, so I figure if they half believe, when we start dating, and I'm not sure which, I can't have all three, she'll be ready, willing, and—"

"Captain."

"I'm sorry, Superintendent. Being a celebrity is fun."

"I did not interrupt to be rude. Muoi is a mere four shops from the photo lab."

"Yep. I see. Jewelry store across the plaza. Crunch time," Binh said, getting to his feet. "How does this sound? I'll get

202

the guys positioned to move in, then circle around to the side doors."

Kiet approved of Binh's request for approval of his plan. It indicated respect, clear thinking, and hormone evaporation. "I approve."

"You're situated ideally to advance discreetly and cut off a retreat. Two of the guys will be sent in behind you. Superintendent, I do wish you'd carry."

"Carry," Kiet said. "Pack. A piece. As you accurately noted, Captain, it is crunch time, not an appropriate time for debates. Go."

"I'm outta here."

Thirty seconds after Binh was "outta here," Lon Muoi glanced side to side, evidently satisfied that nobody was about to throw a net over him, then walked to Double Happiness Photo. Bolted rather than walked, Kiet noted in mild panic. Muoi had quickstepped the plaza on a direct diagonal, had opened the glass door, yanking the handle hard. An abstract reflection flashed, and Muoi vanished.

Cannot wait for reinforcements, Kiet thought, rushing out of the chocolate shop. Cannot. Two, three, four minutes, until Binh and his men are posted. Cannot permit Muoi to barricade himself. If it is indeed their heroin laboratory, the fortifications will be impressive. Battering in would be difficult, time-consuming. Evidence meanwhile would be flushed down the sewer.

He ran. Foot traffic meandered unpredictably, a nightmare obstacle course. Kiet was not young and never an athlete, but he steered through the shoppers with remarkable speed and grace, bumping lightly when collisions did occur. People who fell were more victims of the cool, slippery marble than the kinetic mass of an outsized Luongan police superintendent.

Fortunately for Kiet, Muoi had swung Double Happiness Photo's door so vigorously that it remained open against a stop. Kiet went in noiselessly, on the toes of his sandals. Muoi was behind the counter, stooping at an inner door, shielded by an unmanned cash register.

A lock clicked, the door moved, and so did Kiet. He slammed into Muoi, threw an arm around his neck, and took him through. The room was hot and bright, illuminated by drying lamps. The astringency of Binh's acetic-whatever burned his eyes. On tables were trays of brownish goo. Working at the tables were three perspiring men. They were naked to the waist and visibly displeased at the intrusion. Burmese, Lao, Thai? He couldn't determine. Nor did it matter, as the man in the middle was cursing in a foreign tongue and reaching under the tables.

Kiet silently cursed his stupid heroism, his impulsiveness. Muoi began to struggle. Kiet tightened his neck hold. The man in the middle produced an automatic rifle. It featured a banana clip and a tubular stock, a weapon design favored by terrorists and cinema commandos. These "cooks" were not of the haute cuisine school, Kiet realized.

Kiet realized, too, that in his scramble from Hickorn Chocolate Depot he had neglected to discard the elephantine, foil-wrapped chocolate bar, which was clutched in his free hand. With a squeeze and twist he adjusted Muoi, his shield, to the cook's gun barrel, jammed the chocolate bar into the small of his back, and relaxed the neck hold so Muoi could speak, not to mention breathe.

Summoning the film noir snarl of his life, he said, "Drop your gun or I'll blow a hole in him you can drive a locomotive through."

"Do it!" Muoi shrieked. "He'll kill me!"

The machine rifle clattered tot he floor. Binh and his officers arrived loudly, wand-waving pistols, yelling for "you motherfuckers" to "freeze." The bravado made Kiet more nervous than the cook-peasant and his machine gun. He had visions of ricocheting bullets and internal bleeding."

"Captain, their arms are raised. Ask your men to secure our prisoners. Please."

Binh motioned them to do so and asked, "What about blubber-butt here?"

Lon Muoi was trembling and the stench of urine blended with the chemical odor. Kiet pushed him away, to Binh, and said, "Yes."

"You're making a mistake," Muoi protested.

"I am?" Kiet said.

"By coincidence, my department and yours broke the case simultaneously. Who could imagine?"

"Your department," Kiet said. "And especially you personally, as Associate Deputy Minister of Defense comma Drug Enforcement Investigation?"

"I apologize to you, Kiet, to you and your people. I owe my loyal staff the humblest of apologies. I will beg their forgiveness on my knees. I'm ambitious. I was seeking glory, trying single-handedly to bust this lab, make a name for myself."

"Eradicating Luong's opium menace entirely by yourself? Commendable."

Lon Muoi shrugged modestly. "You do what you must for your country."

"May I, Superintendent?" Binh asked.

"At your earliest convenience," Kiet said.

Binh took Muoi by the arm and pulled him to his officers and the three cooks, saying "Do same-same, pewk. Up against the wall and spread 'em. Assume the position."

"We're on the same side," Muoi whined. "You're making a big, big mistake."

"No," Kiet said. "I am not. I thank you for saving our lives, although you pleaded strictly for your own. That fellow obeyed. He laid down his weapon. Did he comply because he was in awe of a crime-busting associate deputy minister? I do not believe so. He refrained from killing us because he works for you."

Lon Muoi did not respond. Binh was patting him for

concealed weapons. He said, "Cat's got his tongue, Super-intendent. Whew! Pee-pee City."

"Furthermore," Kiet said. He paused, walked to the door, and removed a key from the lock. A dozen keys and a plump, circular charm were looped on a ring. The charm was so clunky and gaudy Kiet would have thought it a talisman sold in the *Mind*'s classified advertising if he hadn't recognized the BMW logo.

He jangled the keys by Muoi's ear. "Recognize these?"

Muoi's arms were outstretched on the wall. He looked at Kiet and shifted his gaze downward.

"Nothing to say? You are custodian of this foul work-shop and you have nothing to say. The role of stoic martyr does not become you."

Muoi spat on the floor. Kiet resisted the urge to swat him.

"Hey, Superintendent." Binh was exercising with the giant, foil-wrapped chocolate bar as if it were a weight-lifter's dumbbell. "Did I see what I thought I saw? Things were happening fast and furious, but you had the situation under control, and didn't you have them faked out with this sucker?"

"Stupidity," Kiet said, remembering, shuddering. "I should have waited for you."

"Ancient history," Binh said. "C'mon."

Kiet told his tale.

Binh laughed until his eyes watered. "This is fantastic, Superintendent! You nabbed these clowns with a candy bar?"

Kiet was not unaffected by praise, particularly praise that might become legendary, apocrypha repeated at po-lice training classes and cafés. He shrugged modestly.

Binh wand-waved the bar at the suspects, saying "Bang, bang! You're dead. Shot down by a fifty-caliber cocoa cannon."

Goaded by the ridicule, Lon Muoi blurted, "I'll talk to you, Kiet."

"Please do," Kiet said.

"There is a condition. I demand political asylum. Do I have your word of honor that you'll grant me immunity from prosecution and get me safely where I want to go?"

Kiet sighed. "Every criminal in Luong is a political prisoner, so it seems. Which nation, please?"

"Tip Taylor."

26

The uniformed officers escorted the alien chemists to headquarters, two patrolmen instructed to baby-sit, the other two to return to Double Happiness Photo and assist. Kiet's recommendation that the heroin cooks be locked in a vacant cell sans booking was seconded by Binh, who was normally an advocate of due process and the peculiar Mirandization custom he had been taught in America, at their District of Columbia constabulary. The heroin cooks were sullen, in no humor to chat anyway. Every question was answered with a shrug and a pidgin protestation that they did not speak Luongan or French or English, the languages in Kiet and Binh's command. Kiet agreed with Binh's evaluation of them as "lying sacks of shit," and that their silence was no hindrance at the moment, but a happy virtue, because they seemed resolved to reveal nothing to anybody.

Binh and Kiet had tunneled into the mother lode of Luongan heroin. It was theirs. But they needed time to decide what to do with their booty.

Associate Deputy Minister Muoi was perhaps in a humor

to chat, but eye contact between Binh and Kiet, a wink by the former, said not yet, not in the best interests of law enforcement psychology. Let the bastard stew in his own juices for a while, the juices being, Binh suggested to Kiet with a nudge and a grin and a whisper, the dark blotch on his Hong Kong tailored slacks.

Binh had ordered Muoi to a chair, had ordered him to *sit*, as if he were a domestic animal. Binh then switched off the heat lamps and turned up the air-conditioning, thus chilling their prisoner's thighs and especially his crotch. Kiet knew he should chastise Binh, but he didn't. He was not punishing Muoi for opium trafficking, he was punishing him because he had been born rich and Binh had not. Class struggle, Kiet thought. Shiherazade and Festerra and Ril Thoi had no monopoly on it. Envy was universal, apolitical.

The superintendent's adjutant was a prankster, not a sadist, so Kiet did not interfere with the lad's sophomoric fun. Lon Muoi was left to shiver and to worry while they searched the laboratory.

Double Happiness Photo was, as Kiet had suspected, a fortress. The outside exit was secured by steel bars and the windows were painted black, shuttered, and locked. Legitimate photographic film developing and printing equipment occupied one-third of the room. It appeared to be in current use, probably producing just enough wedding pictures and tourist snapshots to make the shop credible as a criminal front operation.

Double Happiness Photo's nonphotographic business was impressive. Kilogram-size, plastic-bound bricks of Luong White No. 1 were stacked in a pyramid under the table from which the cook had withdrawn his weapon. Kiet counted thirty-seven bricks. Heaped beneath the adjacent tables were rice-flour bags. They were plump with a white powder. On them was printed the logo of Lon Muoi, the wealthy rice wholesaler and miller, father of his son, Lon Muoi, the bureaucrat and heroin trafficker.

Binh slit a bag, inserted a fingertip, licked it, and said that anybody baking fortune cookies with the stuff was in for the shock of a lifetime. He hefted the bag, estimating five keys, maybe six. Eleven to thirteen pounds of pure horse, he said, whistling. Kiet counted sixty-five sacks of mock rice flour. He scribbled calculations on notepaper. Five point five (the average of five and six) multiplied by sixty-five. Add thirty-seven. Three hundred and ninety-five kilos, the shy side of four hundred. Four hundred kilograms of heroin. Eight hundred eighty pounds of heroin.

"Look at the cookware, Superintendent," Binh said, gesturing. "Barely half the trays contain base. Those big pots over there are cleaned up and those empty charcoal bags, I'm reckoning they've cooked about all the base they have in inventory. They're gonna move some product!"

"How much production?" Kiet asked. "In terms of time."

"Ten days. Two weeks, three at the outside. That's just a wild guess. They're cranked for volume. Jesus, Superintendent, stretch those numbers out and this Mickey Mouse little cookhouse is manufacturing ten to fifteen metric tons per year. By statistics I remember, that's around twenty-five percent of Golden Triangle annual output."

"Substantial," Kiet said.

"Yeah, and they've just recently got into high gear. Imagine what Hickorn's gonna be like a year from now if we don't get a handle on the situation."

"Unpleasant imagining," Kiet said.

"You got that right, Superintendent. Lemme figure something."

Binh was performing computations on Kiet's notepaper. The arithmetic function was multiplication and the numbers contained many zeros. Kiet asked what he was doing.

"Street value," Binh said.

"Excuse me?"

"You know, if there's a humongous drug bust in New

York or Miami, they find a load in a ship or something, they hold a press conference. Well, they don't say it's X pounds of X percent pure this or that."

"Of course not," said the baffled Kiet.

"What they do is figure what it'll cost on the retail level, what the junkie on the street'll have to shell out after the drug's been distributed and cut umpteen times. The bigger the value of the bust, the better the arresting agency looks. Tom Brokaw and Dan Rather whip a bottom line on you that'll definitely grab your attention."

Binh frowned and began erasing. "Three trillion six hundred billion. Yeah, we're talking big time, but three trillion six ain't kosher. Must be I screwed up on the decimal point."

"Later," Kiet said. "Please examine these slips."

"A photo stub like the one at Vinnie's that turned you on to Double Happiness Photo. Hey, the same five-digit number!"

"Indeed."

"Same number as Vinnie's stub?"

Kiet took it from a pocket and compared. "Yes."

Binh snapped his fingers. "Sure, that's gotta be the pass. The people dropping off film, the few legit customers this slimepit has, their stubs are in sequence, no two the same. But you bop in with—three-six-seven-four-two— and you're eligible for special service. Did you see the buzzer on the front counter? Saves hiring a salesclerk. Push the buzzer. Somebody comes out. Whip the magic number on him, pay your money, pick up your h."

"The single-kilo packages and the pseudorice sacks," Kiet said. "A diverse marketing approach."

"Yeah. My feeling is that one-key units were made available to local small fry."

"To pay overhead and finance a Hickorn heroin infrastructure," Kiet said.

"Right on. Peddle ten, fifteen, twenty keys a week, that's a pretty fair piece of walking-around change."

Binh hefted a rice sack, glared at Lon Muoi, and continued, "As far as I'm concerned, this is the heavy-duty action, the export commodity. Hey, Muoi, does your father know you pack heroin in his bags? I'll bet he doesn't. He's an honorable man. He'd disown you, he knew what kind of happy horseshit you were up to your slimy gills in."

Muoi's knees were locked, hands clasped in a vee between his thighs. He looked at Kiet and said, "I'll talk to you, Kiet. I refuse to talk to your peon."

Binh's mouth gaped. Kiet's hands raised. Binh rolled his eyes. Kiet said, "Talk. I am listening."

"Immunity and asylum," Muoi said. "That was our bargain. Protect me and I'll talk. Not until."

Kiet shook his head no and started to pace, hands clasped behind his back. An excellent technique for disquieting suspects, Kiet knew. It looked good in the movies and would in this instance burn chocolate calories.

Muoi's body remained immobile, though his eyes scanned Kiet. Splendid, he thought, continuing until Binh cleared his throat and began tapping a foot.

Kiet sighed theatrically and said, "Mr. Muoi, we have no bargain. We have only a demand. Your ludicrous demand. Allow me to remind you, please, that you swallowed my telephoned bait."

Binh smiled. "Hook, line, and sinker."

"You can't prove it, Kiet. It's your word against mine."

"Guess again, Muoi. We tape-recorded the conversation," Binh lied.

Muoi gulped. "You're lying," he said without authority.

An ingenious lie, thought Kiet, who rattled the BMW key ring and said, "The tape as an evidence exhibit. The door key on your ring as an evidence exhibit. Those two exhibits alone will convict you. They are incontrovertible. An easy case for a prosecutor, an impossibility for a defense attorney."

"The jury'll be out five minutes, max," Binh said, nodding assuredly.

213

Muoi stared silently downward.

"Of course—" Kiet said, hesitating.

"Of course what?" Muoi asked eagerly.

"Of course, life isn't precisely scripted. What is the expression, Captain?"

"Gray area," Binh said. "As opposed to black and white."

"Thank you. Gray area. Compromise. Extenuating circumstances. We are reasonable men. You loosen your position, we shall loosen ours."

"My loosening depends on your proposal."

"I propose that you answer a few innocuous questions. No initial reference to opium."

"I—I suppose so."

"Splendid. Why defection to Tip Taylor?"

"He's my best American friend," Muoi said easily. "He has clout. I'll have to leave Luong forever if you have your way with me, Kiet. Tip can do things for me and I trust him."

"Trust him? You trust a man whose computer you infected with bacteria?"

"Virus, Superintendent."

"Whatever."

"Tip told me about his ECOSIT program," Muoi said. "It was a terrible shame, but you have no proof—"

"Who else in Luong but the bright, young Lon Muoi has the technical skill? Nobody. Who else but the precocious Lon Muoi could bug Cuong Van's office, pretend to remove all bugs after they were discovered, but leave two of four in place? Nobody!"

"You're dreaming, Kiet."

Kiet stopped pacing. He crouched, his face millimeters from Muoi's, clasped his knees for support, and said, "Lately my dreams have been nightmares. You are a major cause, muchacho."

Muoi looked at him.

214

Kiet smiled a fatherly smile and repeated, "Muchacho. Kiddo."

"On tape too," Binh added. "You and the Red Baron. This afternoon. In its entirety."

"How?"

"No way, José," Binh said. "Classified information."

"I see no harm," Kiet said. "The departed member of the Three Stooges altered you from bugor to bugee. Your reason for bugs *and* viruses, please."

"I am a patriot," Muoi said.

"Jesus," Binh said.

"I am! I admit I'm ambitious. I'm not a complete innocent. I knew that except for family influence I never would have been appointed associate deputy minister of defense, drug enforcement investigation. Minister Van and his general staff excluded me from the decision-making process whenever they could. They'd schedule meetings when I was out of the office. I was treated like a child, Kiet. To do my job, to make my boughten title a meaningful job, I had to learn important policy developments through an earphone. I was humiliated. Not a day went by that I didn't lose face."

Muoi finished speaking and lowered his head. His eyes were moist, his complexion pale, his expression morose. The performance almost convinced Kiet, who wondered if Muoi's dilettante education included drama lessons.

"Tyler Polk Taylor's computer virus. Why?"

"Do you know what ECOSIT stands for?"

"I was told the acronym. I forget."

"Elimination of COntrolled Substance Infiltration and Trafficking. But you know what *ecosit* is in Luongan. Violation of a restaurant sanitation law. People laugh behind Tip's back. He doesn't know. He doesn't know because he doesn't speak Luongan.

"His goal is to head the Golden Triangle opium war, but he can't bother to learn Asian languages and Asian customs. He doesn't respect me or any Asian drug enforce-

215

ment leader. I programmed the virus into ECOSIT to wound but not cripple him. I broke the password on my office computer and modem in ten minutes and ruined the program in ten more. He thinks Asians are stupid and backward gooks, so he didn't safeguard his system against virus attacks. Do you understand what I am pouring from my heart to you, Kiet?"

"You are a wellspring of nationalistic pride?"

"Yes," Muoi said, solemnly as a wedding vow.

"Yet Taylor is your trusted friend?"

"I idolized him at the beginning. He's from Kennebunkport. His father plays golf with Gerald Ford and Bob Hope. Ambassador Smithson is his father-in-law. My family is prominent in Luong. Tip is an American nobleman. He was a revered older brother to me. He used me most cleverly."

"I recall him speaking highly of you," Kiet said. "Several days ago at the airport. How did he use you most cleverly?"

"Uh, that's not an innocuous question."

"Very well," Kiet said. "I'll answer for you. For reasons yet unknown, Tip Taylor suffered selective blindness. Souvang Zhu's opium activities were invisible to him. You are Luong's ranking opium official. You cooperated in the invisibility by preventing information from reaching Cuong Van and myself. You also spied on Cuong Van and announced opium missions in advance."

Lon Muoi did not speak, did not emote.

"We're far beyond narcotics conspiracy, Mr. Associate Deputy Minister. Selling Ministry of Defense secrets is a treasonable offense."

"Sandbags," Binh said pleasantly. "A pole. Rope. Blindfold. A last cigarette."

"I didn't sell information," Muoi shouted. "I don't need money!"

"Your motivation was patriotic, then?"

216

Muoi regained self-control and looked away. Is my breath so foul? Kiet wondered.

"Next question," he said. "Why did Air Vice-Marshal Zhu and his fighter planes attack us? Answer. To kill us. Next question, multiple parts. Why? And who? Captain Binh and myself? Or the Cuban Festerra? Or all three of us?"

"Whom," Binh said.

"Answer," Kiet said. "All three of us. Alberto Festerra was the principal target. Festerra and the Bolsheviks and the American gangster were opium competitors. Captain Binh and I were nuisances. How does that saying go, Captain, three birds in hand are worth more than one in the bush?"

"Something like that, Superintendent."

"Hickorn police officers and a Communist together. Very convenient. We were in cahoots."

"How did you survive?" Muoi said. "There were stories."

"Elvis and his UFO buddies," Binh said. "They made the scene like the cavalry in a Duke Wayne flick."

"Not funny," Muoi said.

Kiet leaned in, his nose touching Muoi's. He hoped his breath *was* foul. "Being strafed is not funny. You talk to us, son. I have no further patience."

"Tip—"

"Yes, yes. I will contact him. No promises, however."

"Your questions and answers are on the mark," Muoi said.

"Your motivation, please? Patriotism?"

"Yes, but I'm not going to elaborate. I'm in over my head. I need time to think."

Muoi's head was in his hands. Kiet gave him a fatherly shoulder pat, stood, and asked, "A final question, please. You must answer, not I. Who killed Yung Lim?"

"Who?"

"Little Big Vinnie Jones's employee. Jones. The American gangster."

217

"I don't know."

"Who killed Little Big Vinnie?"

Muoi's jaw fell. "You're kidding."

Kiet read Muoi's surprise as authentic. He took Binh aside and said, "The lad has a monstrous inferiority complex."

"I noticed, and I love it," Binh whispered. "Nifty interrogation job, Superintendent. You going in for the kill? He's emotional Jell-O right now."

"I am uneasy."

"In what respect?"

"Muoi has divulged some facts."

"More to come," Binh said. "Film at eleven. Go for it, Superintendent."

"I believe he is patriotic, if extremely deluded. I believe there are voids in his knowledge."

"How do you suggest we fill said voids?"

"This is a heroin laboratory," Kiet said.

"Understatement of the century," Binh said. "Hey, I think I know where you're coming from!"

Kiet shushed him.

"Sorry. We'll resume business as usual. A sting operation. The rice bags filled like that, you can bet your sweet ass we'll have paying customers coming out of our ears."

"Indeed."

Binh snapped his fingers. "Oops, we can't throw a party without the hosts. I guess I should bring back the cooks."

"Yes," Kiet said. "But bring with the hosts an additional guest."

27

Kiet's additional guest yawned and said, "Your adjutant awakened me from the soundest sleep I've had in weeks, Bosha, but I'd accept a year of insomnia for what you're showing me. This is wonderful."

Minister of Defense Cuong Van's yawn triggered another, Kiet's. "A nocturnal hour, yes, now that you remind me."

"The arcade stores are closed. Do you expect heroin buyers tonight?"

Kiet glanced at a wall clock: thirteen minutes past two. "No, Cuong. Anybody wandering about the plaza would draw attention to himself. He would be either challenged or reported to the police by the security guards. The photo retrieval stubs numbered three-six-seven-four-two tell me that the trafficking occurs during normal hours. I visualize gentlemen wearing business suits and military uniforms and false respectability, nonchalantly carrying briefcases, briefcases large enough to accommodate six-kilo sacks of heroin."

Cuong Van looked at the three heroin cooks retrieved

from jail and the policemen guarding them, and shook his head angrily. "I presume these chemists double as salesclerks. They and their clients are brazen scoundrels, Bosha. They come and go in the middle of Hickorn like accountants taking ledgers to clients."

"Past tense," Kiet said. "Hopefully. With any degree of good fortune."

Van yawned and said, "You've always claimed that you don't believe in luck, Bosha."

Kiet yawned and said, "At this moment I shall believe in whatever believes in me."

Van pointed at the cooks, who were consenting at gunpoint to fill empty Lon Muoi rice flour bags with rice flour scooped from one-hundred-kilo sacks balanced on hand trucks. "The strangest part of Captain Binh's request that I join you, Bosha, was that I haul along half a ton of flour. My staff is accustomed to my unorthodox and unreasonable demands, but being ordered to army mess halls in the middle of the night to requisition rice flour has them thoroughly confused."

"I appreciate the effort," Kiet said. "Luong appreciates the effort."

"It makes more sense now," Van said.

"The old switcheroo," said Binh, who stood stiffly at the periphery of the discussion.

Van peered around him to a chair in the corner and a glum Lon Muoi.

"Much as I want to, I can't go over and say anything to him," Van said, his face tight with rage. "I might shoot him. We knew he was doing something, but—selling heroin in bags stamped with his father's name . . ."

"He figured no one would question a notable brand name, sir, and rip into the bags to check, sir," Binh said.

"He professes an unspecified patriotic motive," Kiet said.

"He and his partner, Zhu?"

"Yes."

"What are they up to?"

"I don't think young Muoi has an inkling, Cuong, not in the sense that the desired result will match the actual."

Cuong Van smiled and yawned. "Bosha, you have a gift for ornately wrapped words. What in the hell are you saying?"

Kiet yawned, then summarized his interrogation of Lon Muoi and the discovery of Little Big Vinnie Jones's body.

"Russians?" Van asked, squinting. "Cubans, Ril Thoi and the Rouge, American mobsters, senior ministry and air force men, *and* Ambassador Smithson's son-in-law. Who else is peddling opium in Hickorn?"

Kiet yawned again. "Elvis?"

"No, at least not today or the past several days," Van said, yawning. "Stop that. No, Elvis has an alibi. He and his friends are orbiting Saturn."

"Ah," Kiet said.

"My secret is out," Van said, shrugging. "I'm a compulsive *Mind* reader. I can't control myself."

Kiet gestured to the flour sacks. Inspired by gun barrels that followed their backs as if on strings, the opium chemist trio was working with an urgency that suggested sandbags to counter a monsoon flood.

"I will not go ahead unless you approve, Cuong."

"How closely does rice flour resemble heroin, Captain?" Van asked Binh.

"Fairly close in regard to color and weight, sir," Binh said. "The texture's different. Good flour's much finer, and Lon Muoi Senior's grade is tops. Heroin the buyers are accustomed to receiving out of this lab is sort of grainy."

"So our substitute would pass a cursory perusal of the sacks, but not a sample test?"

"No way, sir. The sort of animals you can figure they're selling to, they're not likely to take anybody's word, even their old buddy Zhu's. They'll dip into a bag, run it across fingertips, and taste. The seller is gonna be dead meat."

221

"A moral dilemma," Kiet said to Van. "A quandary. Please help me decide properly."

"I think I'm reading your mind, Bosha. That dilemma is the choice of arresting buyers when they pay their money and receive heroin or selling them rice flour and letting their customers deal with them."

"Indeed," Kiet said.

"A sting operation versus the royal shaft," Binh offered.

"You're sly, Bosha. You're influencing my decision by preparing the ersatz heroin. 'The work is done, Cuong,' you are saying. 'We can go either way. Say the word.'"

"Guilty," Kiet confessed. "Lives may be lost and we would be de facto executioners."

"Your conscience needs company," Van said.

"Yes."

"Mine too. I know how you're leaning, Bosha, genius that I am. Cast your vote."

"Excuse me for evading your demand, Cuong. Souvang Zhu?"

"Taking him into custody with troops?"

"Yes. An arrest by my department is out of the question. We haven't the manpower or weaponry."

"Would he and could he set a coup d'état in motion if I tried? Yes and yes."

"You guys—gentlemen, you're amazing, this clairvoyance thing you zap back and forth," Binh said.

"Could you take him quietly, by surprise?"

"No," Van said without hesitation. "Zhu is a wastrel, a man about town with the ladies, but he's smart and alert. He watches his backside and has friends in the armed forces I'm probably not aware of."

"Would you win?"

"Yes, but bloodily. Zhu enjoys strong army support in Obon, Bosha. As a prominent opium bandit, he and the Second Military District have much in common. Obon troops and his fighter command would cut the country in half. We would prevail eventually, though at the cost of a civil war."

"Do I know how you are leaning, Cuong?"

"Answer this, Bosha. Are you absolutely convinced Zhu is what you say he is?"

"Yes, ninety-nine percent. My one-percent uncertainty will be clarified by observing who—whom comes to our heroin market."

"Then you know how I am leaning. You also know that as a soldier I have been trained to confront enemies face-to-face."

"Battles," Kiet said. "Foxholes, bayonets, combat."

"Don't be melodramatic, Bosha."

"Sorry."

"You confront your enemies directly too, Bosha. You walk up to a man and look into his eyes when you arrest him, do you not?"

"Yes."

"All right, have you last-second reservations about our sneaky option?"

"No," Kiet said. "If I do at the final instant, I shall go to Luong University Hospital and visit Bao Canh, son of Quin."

"It's settled. I'm going to get rid of the trays on the tables and take a nap," Van said.

"Go home," Kiet said. "I will rotate surveillance teams and notify you when the heroin is sold."

Van shook his head no. "I wouldn't miss it."

"The cooks are doing nice work," Binh said. "Assholes and elbows. They'll wrap up mucho pronto."

Van looked at Binh. "Where is your interpreter, Bosha?"

"Alas, my budget does not permit."

Binh blushed, highly flattered that his idols were kidding him.

"I'll clear the trays with you," Kiet said.

"Never mind," Van said. "I'd rather reminisce and drink coffee. I'm not sleepy."

223

Nor am I all of a sudden, Kiet thought. Their joint decision, however justified, had decreed death. They might as well have worn judicial robes and signed warrants.

Neither man yawned again.

28

Five days later, at the luxuriant park adjacent to the street at which Kiet and Binh had staged their Scarlet Mongoose raid, two men sat on a bench, lackadaisically tossing crumbs from their sandwiches to a swarm of crowned pigeons.

The men occupied opposite ends of the bench, an appropriate gap for adult male strangers. Each was tall and distinguished, but noteworthy in different ways.

One was a Luongan. He was bulky and widely known to Hickornians. Due to his recent familiarity with extraterrestrial creatures, he was a metaphysical celebrity to the impressionable.

The other was a Caucasian American. He was lanky, visibly distressed, and even taller than the Asiatic.

The strangers had an unmistakable kinship: jackknifed knees. The stubby benches had been engineered by average-size Luongans for average-size Luongans.

"They're disgusting," said the American. "The ubiquitous pigeon. A worldwide nuisance."

The Luongan looked at the statue of Prince Savhana.

What had initially appeared to be whitish shoulder epaulets and peacock headdress were not. A disgrace, he thought. Our hero of heroes deserves his own guano patrol.

"You're lobbing too much in, too fast, fattening somebody's meal," he cautioned. "You don't like your lunch?"

"To tell you the truth, I'm not overly hungry," said the American.

The truth would be nice, the Luongan thought. "Don't give it to them all at once. They become greedy and frenzied."

"An allegorical comment regarding Luong, opium, and associated subjects?" Tyler Polk (Tip) Taylor asked.

Bamsan Kiet did not reply. He had resisted the desire to confront Taylor immediately following the heroin adventure, had awaited the drug enforcement adviser's overture. Aside from depositing Lon Muoi at dawn at the U.S. Embassy—in handcuffs—he had kept silent. On Kiet's recommendation, Cuong Van had kept silent. His Royal Highness Prince Novisad Pakse concurred. Thus the official Luongan reaction was utter silence.

Kiet knew that Taylor would come to him in time, and when he did he would be desperate. Using a junior cultural attaché as a messenger boy, Taylor had approached Kiet this morning at headquarters. Kiet had sent the courier away, saying perhaps. The lad returned, citing urgency. Kiet dispatched him, saying oh, very well. He returned, requesting that the meeting be clandestine. Kiet instructed him to advise his superior that he would have no more of cathedrals and aching knees. Whatever you say, the messenger informed Kiet, who said splendid; we shall have our covert rendezvous at a favorite park of mine; lunch is on you.

"Superintendent, did you hear me?"

Jaws at full extension, Kiet bit into his sandwich. Inside the split French loaf was lettuce, tomato, onion, condiments, ham, roast beef, sausages, cheeses, and meatballs. Kiet had never before seen nor tasted such a delight. The

American Embassy kitchen prepared the sandwiches, which Taylor termed "submarines," despite no detectable seafood.

Kiet patiently chewed, then said, "I heard you."

"Are you being deliberately obstinate?"

"Yes."

Taylor sighed heavily. "Well, I can't fault your negative opinion of me, you and your Major Dinh. As they say, if you dance, you have to pay the fiddler."

"Yes."

Taylor said, "I asked to see you partly because my only version of that Double Happiness situation is Lon Muoi's."

"We moved him to headquarters during the night," Kiet said. "He would not know everything."

"Were handcuffs really and truly necessary, Superintendent? At that ungodly hour?"

"Yes."

"You were making a statement, weren't you? I.e., this criminal scum individual wants you and that's fine and dandy with us? He is a nonperson, as are my colleagues and I. Not in my lifetime will I understand you people."

"You understand perfectly," Kiet said.

"Well," Taylor said, licking an index finger and daubing thin air. "Score one for me. No arrests were made public, but as Lon related your advantageous deployment in the photo lab to me, it would be like shooting fish in a rain barrel."

"We spoke quietly and in Mr. Muoi's presence and did not consult him. He knows nothing. No arrests were made."

"So I feared. While you didn't confide in him, you didn't blindfold him either. He witnessed the rice flour folderol. Who bought the counterfeit drugs?"

"Regular customers," Kiet said. "Our prisoners worked so commendably hard that they had time to prepare small bags too. Petty amateur traffickers, local thugs, foreign habitués of the Strip who supported themselves dealing

227

modest quantities. No murders have been reported to us this week, so I must presume our patrons learned of the fraud before retailing the goods and, further, deduced that they were themselves fraud victims of the proper authorities rather than their peers, and did not seek vengeance."

"I'm referring to the large packages."

"Ah," Kiet said. "The money received was gratifying. All hard currencies. We transferred the cash to the Royal Treasury. The minister of finance was euphoric. He said that because of the monetary infusion we may not have a balance-of-payments deficit this year."

Taylor winked. "Have your fun, Superintendent. Reveal what you will reveal at your speed. Twist your knife. Lord knows, your torment is trifling compared to what I have endured from my own people."

"Excuse me?"

"No. That juicy tidbit is the finale. Curious? *Après vous*, chum."

"Very well. Air Vice-Marshal Zhu's minions came in throughout the day. Fighter command pilots and enlisted men, shutterbug hobbyists all. The last parcel was picked up two hours before sundown. Our cooperative chemist-clerks told us that pickups were usually less concentrated, one or two per day, but a big transaction had been arranged with new bandit leadership. They were vague, but I interpreted it as a formation of a consortium, a group newly organized and strong enough to reestablish stability to the trade. Opium bandits and fighter planes, an unbeatable combination. The Mustangs departed Hickorn International forty-five minutes prior to nightfall."

"Who?"

Kiet shrugged. "Whom, I don't know, but my best guess is some of the same bandit chieftains in new alliances."

"Where?"

"I thought you could tell me."

"Our spy satellites have mapped every square inch

228

within the radius range of those aircraft. It's as if they disappeared into the Bermuda Triangle."

"Where?"

Tip Taylor raised aristocratic eyebrows. "You haven't heard of the apocryphal Bermuda Triangle? Several weeks ago the Bermuda Triangle was the cover story in the *Hickorn Enquiring Mind*. Some balderdash about the lost continent of Atlantis and Martin Bormann. Not that I am a recreational reader, mind you. But you never know what you might glean from a printed page. I study it in an intelligence-gathering mode."

"Intelligence," Kiet mumbled. "Oxymoron City."

"Lon Muoi is driving us mad, Superintendent Kiet. He rants and raves and makes outrageous demands. He's a spoiled child. I didn't previously comprehend the extent of his self-centeredness."

"What demands, please?"

"Landed immigrant status in America is the tune I hear endlessly, number one on his Hit Parade."

"Will you grant him political asylum?"

"We were equivocal on the subject until I was subpoenaed by a secret Senate subcommittee suddenly formed to investigate the—situation. Ever try to obtain legal advice on a transpacific telephone connection? My ears are still ringing from the static."

"Like calling across the street in Hickorn," Kiet said sympathetically. "Subpoenaed?"

"An apt comparison. I hope I didn't misinterpret anything in the static. My attorneys urged me to book him on the same plane and don't let him out of my sight. They feel that he'll be a beneficial witness. His perspective as a Luongan, his political leanings—he'll relate to the subcommittee in a manner I cannot. They'll relate his patriotism to my—what is alleged to have been done by me—participation. We're assembling travel papers for him. Thank the good Lord, I can still pull a string or three.

229

Since the object of the secret session is to jump the gun on the media, I might be able to buy a tiny edge."

"Subpoenaed?" Kiet said. "Witness? Subcommittee? Session? Media?"

"The finale," Taylor said, winking. "The last act."

"I have said what there is to say about Double Happiness Photo. I wasn't surprised at the extent of the heroin trade. Are you, sir?"

"No," Taylor said, exhaling the word in abject defeat. "No surprises. Muoi prattled on, naming Communists and American gangsters. Lies, lies, lies. We've sketched a rough picture of how Ril Thoi, the Soviets, and that Cuban networked in the situation. Although they acted out an unintentional Marx Brothers movie, it doesn't necessarily follow that they couldn't have made hay in event of a governmental collapse.

"I believe Muoi was counting on the United States to step in militarily. He was leveraging himself in the event his asylum application was disapproved. He could lose himself in the shuffle."

"The anonymity of a bloodbath," Kiet said.

"A horrifying contingency."

"You knew Muoi was lying because you knew who the heroin purchasers were," Kiet said.

"I wasn't privy to the mechanics of the situation, so technically I didn't know. The Double Happiness Photo terminus was a mystery to me, ignorance being bliss, if you will."

"I will," Kiet said. "Muoi and Zhu were your layers of insulation between ideological purity and day-to-day business?"

"Well stated," Taylor said.

"You may be mildly interested to learn that we have probably solved the Vincent Jones and Yung Lim murders."

"Mildly is the operative modifier, Superintendent. Forgive me, but my situation is on a different level than guns and gangsters."

"Not so great a distinction, sir. Not so rarefied. By vanishing into your Bermuda Triangle, Marshal Zhu and his fighter pilots essentially made orphans of their enlisted personnel. Many questions are being asked and their father figures are gone forever. Gather these lads in a room and the pointed fingers resemble a bony thicket. The consensus is that the dedicated enlisted man who got the call through that phone we bugged, the crucial Zhu and Muoi conversation, ingratiated himself further by zotzing Jones and Lim, who showed exactly enough inclination to be serious opium players to die. Forgive me, sir, but from the perspective of being strafed, Zhu and his Mustang aerial gun platforms personify gangsterism."

"Zotzing? What is zotzing?"

"Crime lingo for a professional hit," Kiet said. "Tie the gangsters and the fighter aces and Mr. Muoi and his electronic shenanigans together, *Papaver somniferum* the ribbon, and you have a neat package. Tell me, please, how you fit in? Or do you prefer that I tell you?"

"I'm being recalled permanently," Taylor said. "That saves Luong the bother of expelling me and us the embarrassment. Hickorn is becoming hazardous to my health as it is. Dad-Dad, uh, my father-in-law, Ambassador Smithson, and I have been on frigid terms this week. The understatement of the year is that he's out of sorts with me. He has determined that since I was running a political operation on my own that I am incorrigibly sneaky. Ergo, I have been unfaithful to him professionally; I have been unfaithful to Edwina, my beloved wife. Dad-Dad's paramount marital concern is disease. Do not be offended, Superintendent, but Luongan hygiene is not what it might be."

"Of course I am not offended. Venereal disease is epidemic among Luongan womanhood," Kiet said. "Such is life."

231

Taylor pinked. "Oh, my God!"

"You didn't know?" Kiet asked, his fury caged inside gentle words and a tight smile. "Luongan ladies are infected with all the strains."

"I see," Taylor said, winking and smirking humorlessly. "Score one for you. Twisting the ol' knife. Disemboweling me with sarcasm. The ambassador had a smidgen too much to drink at a reception yesterday. He challenged me to a duel: sabers or pistols. My choice. Isn't that sporting of him? So what can an investigative committee do to me, eh?"

"We have not gotten to why, Mr. Taylor."

"You offered to answer your own question," Taylor said, tossing it out with a jerk of the wrist, as if to the pigeons. "Be my guest."

"The Third Force," Kiet said. "What you told me in the cathedral."

"A trial balloon."

"You and Zhu and Muoi were financing your Third Force with funds received from heroin. When the opium war brought down His Royal Highness, the forces of righteousness would be monetarily and militarily mighty. There would be no power vacuum for Ril Thoi and his ilk to fill."

"So far, so good."

"Impure ideology was your downfall. Greed overruled politics. Not you, not young Muoi. Souvang Zhu. My Captain Binh, Major Dinh to you, said Zhu was having menstrual cycles, a figurative monthly curse, I presume."

Tip Taylor chuckled. "Male menopause. Midlife crisis. Six of one, half a dozen of the other. Souvang was a textbook study. The clothes, the weight loss, the girls. I should have had my head examined. Monday morning quarterbacking it, Zhu didn't give a whit about Luong's future. He cared how many sexual conquests he could manage per night."

"Zhu was entrusted with the heroin proceeds?"

232

"He held the kitty. He took the risks and made the deals, so we couldn't tactfully demand the kind of accountability in hindsight we should have demanded. We would be insulting him, causing loss of face. Souvang supplied Hickorn bank deposit receipts. On the surface, they seemed clearly laundered and faithful to our mission. We couldn't spot-check without compromising ourselves. Those receipts are proving to be bogus."

"Swiss banks?" Kiet asked.

"No. Ever since the situation blew up in my face, we've been trying to chase the money down. Souvang's quote-unquote investments are not quite so conservative as Swiss banks. He squandered a prodigious amount locally, on wine, women, and the occasional song. And in bonus payments to his fighter command airmen. Bribes and payments for criminal deeds, as it were."

"That was vaguely mentioned in our sessions with them," Kiet said. "How much money, can you estimate?"

Taylor shook his head. "Millions and millions and millions. Yankee dollars, Superintendent, not zin."

"Where is the balance of the money?"

"Hong Kong is the general consensus. This morning we analyzed a couple of blips and got lucky. A fabulous villa. Four million U.S. dollars. In cash. Cars and furnishings and a concubine are in the process of being delivered."

"He was building a nest," Kiet said. "Imminent retirement."

"That's our current evaluation."

"Your objective strikes me as cloudy," Kiet said.

"No, it is—was crystal clear, possibly too simplistic and clear."

"Opium and communism lead us to violent anarchy. His Royal Highness and Minister of Defense Cuong Van are unable to cope. Your Third Force fund is introduced. You buy the loyalty of the armed forces and additional supplies as required."

"Augmented by mercenaries."

Kiet suppressed a groan and stood. "Mercenaries?"

"Pay a man a wage to do a job and he does it," Taylor said. "The toil of an efficient body and a mind uncluttered by politics."

Kiet inserted the uneaten submarine sandwich portion into the brown paper sack in which it had been brought, thinking *dinner*. "Your last act, please. Your finale."

"You heard the verbal."

"And?"

Tip Taylor got up and extended a hand. There were wrinkles in his clothing and his ramrod posture was gone.

"Just the physical," he said. "Getting on the airplane."

29

"Hundreds of channels, Bosha. Television programming from every corner of the world. If I were not seeing with my own two eyes, I would not believe."

Bosha. Kiet blushed. To be addressed by his ancient nickname by His Royal Highness was the tribute of tributes. "Nor would I, Your Highness."

Kiet, Prince Novisad Pakse, and three others were seated in the television room of the Royal Palace, in cushioned reclining chairs equipped with footrests. The chairs were arranged in an arc facing a forty-five-inch color television receiver. The angle of the chairs to the receiver, the room's lighting, and the acoustics were intended to provide optimum clarity and viewing enjoyment, and the grossly ugly satellite dish on the roof was responsible for the versatility.

Kiet watched, mesmerized, as the octogenarian monarch pushed buttons on a flat keyboard device he called a "remote." The buttons changed the screen selection and the variety seemed infinite.

"A Brazilian soap opera. They're speaking Portuguese, a language we do not."

Kiet wished His Royal Highness hadn't flicked the Brazilians to oblivion so quickly. The leering man with glistening hair was expendable, but the woman, her cleavage—

Prince Pakse pointed at the black people in the Western-style kitchen. The man was making a funny face.

"Bill Cosby. He's hilarious," Prince Pakse said, moving on to a Thai kick-boxing match.

Kiet and his fellow invitees had been in the television room for an hour, delighting with His Royal Highness as he demonstrated the magical technology. British sitcoms, West German soccer, a stolid Moscow news reader, insipid Caucasians of indeterminate nationality squealing and jumping up and down at the sight of an on-stage automobile and refrigerator, a red-faced and silver-haired man shaking a Bible and haranguing the camera, an animated cat chasing an animated mouse, a man dressed in a business suit on a stage interviewing four men dressed in dresses, and on and on.

The television room adjoined the Royal Billiards Room and was the former home of secondary games—a shuffleboard and a snooker table. To a pocket billiards zealot like Prince Pakse, the changeover was no sacrifice.

His Royal Highness had graciously apologized to his guests for neglecting to change clothes before receiving them. He was dressed in a black tuxedo, the uniform of billiards tournaments. It was his custom to wear tuxedos while training, to acclimate himself to a competition environment. He had been practicing for an upcoming tourney in Singapore, he said, and had lost track of the time.

Those who underestimated Luong's ruler derided him in the garment as an emaciated penguin. They did not utter the insult to Prince Pakse's face, nor to Bamsan Kiet's.

The television receiver went blank. His Royal Highness

aimed the remote gadget at a black box, a videocassette recorder. Red lights blinked. The television screen came to life. Men in tuxedos were playing billiards.

"An important nine-ball tournament from Las Vegas," Prince Pakse explained, pushing a button that silenced the commentary. "ESPN telecasted it and I recorded it. I've studied it repeatedly and have learned priceless tips from these professional shooters. I am grateful to ESPN for making it available, and I am grateful to you, Bosha, for eliminating the sin spots on Rue ESPN. May the ghastly Strip soon be a distant memory."

"I cannot take direct credit, Your Highness. The dives are failing because the opium trade is drying up, or at least withering to pre-opium war levels."

"Bosha is too modest, Your Highness," said Minister of Defense Cuong Van. "He deserves the most credit for breaking the back of the heroin industry. That is as direct as direct can be."

"Yes, he does, favorite cousin. But do not deny yourself an ample portion of credit. You men have taken Hickorn out of the heroin business. Now, what is happening to highlands opium?"

"Obon and the countryside is also adjusting to pre-opium war levels," Cuong Van said. "The new generation of bandits is returning to the old ways, the old routes. Drug interdiction people are adapting to the old patterns. I predict that within weeks the new Golden Triangle will be identical to the old, and that Luong will again be an insignificant corner."

Prince Pakse looked at Kiet, who nodded in agreement, then said, "Will the disruption you gentlemen caused affect the quantity of heroin that is smuggled out of Southeast Asia?"

"Perhaps short term," Kiet said. "Long term, no. Not while people stick needles into their arms. Is that a fair assumption, Captain?"

"Yes, sir," said Captain Binh. "Supply and demand,

Your Highness. Unfortunately. We could burn every poppy field in Laos, Burma, Thailand, and, yeah, China too, and the Golden Crescent countries—Iran, Pakistan, and Afghanistan—would pick up the slack. An addict won't stop craving his fix and a pusher won't stop selling it to him."

"Foreign governments have generously assisted us in this mutual problem. Important vacancies exist, however. Should I request replacements?"

Alberto Festerra and Tip Taylor, Kiet thought. The question was asked impassively, but humor lurked in eighty-year-old eyes. He and Binh and Van smiled and shook their heads in unison.

"Your recommendation that we be officially silent and not lodge a formal protest against Mr. Taylor's superiors was brilliant, Bosha. I am doing the same with the Soviets. I am not receiving ambassadors. I am neither returning telephone calls nor written messages.

"We cannot possibly know if there are ramifications in Havana and Moscow, but the Russians are increasing foreign aid, a reliable sign that heads have rolled. They're sending us tractors and prefabricated metal buildings. Their machinery is hardly outside the crates before the engines seize. And what are we to do with metal buildings? Our climate will rust them into a heap of red oxide in no time.

"Those Soviets. They atone in odd, awkward ways. How can you stay angry at the oafs? There is a phrase I don't remember."

"It's the thought that counts," Binh offered.

"Thank you," Prince Pakse said. "Silence is a virtue to Luongans. Why does it unnerve our superpower brothers? Young man, you studied police science in the West, did you not? Have you a theory?"

"Well, sir, Your Highness," said Binh, nervous at being the focus of attention. "I think it's insecurity. If you're not talking, you're automatically angry and they can't, you

238

know, read your feelings and intentions. It's like, you know, when you date an American girl and don't say much, she thinks she's done something wrong and you don't like her or she has bad breath or something."

"Inscrutable," Prince Pakse said, turning to Quin Canh with a warm smile. "You are lucky, to be Bosha's friend."

"Yes, Your Highness."

"How is your son and his musician friends?"

"Improving, Your Highness. Our treatment program is trial and error, but we are improving too."

"You and Luong University are to be commended. It is tragic that we require your dedication, but I am thankful that you're here for us," Prince Pakse said. "Cousin, the Hickorn–Obon highway is once again restricted to armed convoys?"

"Yes, Your Highness," Cuong Van said. "No fighter command, no air cover. The Rouge waylaid a wholesale grocery truck two nights ago and made off with the cargo."

Frozen cakes? Kiet wondered.

"When Zhu wasn't air-freighting narcotics he did hold our old chum Ril Thoi at bay."

"I like the status quo," Cuong Van said. "We can better control who is bound in either direction with what."

"Indisputably," Prince Pakse said, pushing remote buttons. The red lights on the videocassette recorder died and were brought to life on a duplicate machine beside it. The billiards shooters winked off, replaced by Tyler Polk (Tip) Taylor, who was at a table, speaking into a microphone. His clothing and posture and earnestness are immaculate, Kiet observed.

"Unless someone objects, I'll maintain the mute function," Prince Pakse said. "In summary, Mr. Taylor is implicating his chain of command in what the American media is calling LuongGate, beginning with Ambassador Smithson and ending with the President. He was just following orders.

"Lon Muoi hasn't testified before the esteemed senators

yet, but network news shows predict that he will contradict Taylor's allegations. The reporters cannot decide if Muoi is truthful, a pawn, or if he has allied himself with Taylor's bosses. Ah, food!"

Servants rolled in a buffet cart and placed metal trays and paper plates on everybody's lap. Prince Pakse switched back to the nine-ball tournament and said, "TV trays, disposable chinaware, good food, and television, a Western custom I could readily adopt. Bosha, don't be bashful."

Kiet took a handful of raw vegetables and said, "Thank you anyway, Your Highness, but I am on a diet."

Quin scooped fried shrimp, rice, and a pastry onto Kiet's plate, and said, "Leave the wild stories for Taylor and Muoi, Bamsan. Eat."

Kiet ate.